MW01294675

# Spiritual Marriage
## The Curse of Illicit Sexual Union

*by*
## EBENEZER GYASI

Bloomington, IN  Milton Keynes, UK

authorHOUSE

*First published by AuthorHouse 5/24/2006*

*ISBN: 1-4208-6895-0 (sc)*

*Printed in the United States of America*
*Bloomington, Indiana*

*This book is printed on acid-free paper.*

Scriptures are quoted from the King James Version of the Bible unless otherwise noted.

Scripture marked MSG taken from *The Message.* Copyright © 1993, 1994, 1995, 1996, 2000, 2001, 2002. Used by permission of NavPress Publishing Group.

Scripture quotations marked NASB are taken from the New American Standard Bible®. Copyright © 1960, 1962, 1963, 1968, 1971, 1972, 1973, 1975, 1977, 1995 by The Lockman Foundation. Used by permission. (www.Lockman.org)

Scripture quotations marked AMP are taken from the Amplified® Bible. Copyright © 1954, 1958, 1962, 1964, 1965, 1987 by The Lockman Foundation Used by permission. (www.Lockman.org)

Scripture quotations marked NLT are taken from **New Living Translation** Holy Bible. Copyright © 1996 by Tyndale Charitable Trust. Used by permission of Tyndale House Publishers.

Scripture marked NIV is taken from the HOLY BIBLE, NEW INTERNATIONAL VERSION®. Copyright © 1973, 1978, 1984 International Bible Society. Used by permission of Zondervan. All rights reserved.

Spiritual Marriage
&
The Curse of Illicit Sexual Union

© ***Deliverance-On-The-Go Ministries 2005:*** *The seed of your future is in your vision!*

Ebenezer Gyasi
Deliverance-On-The-Go Ministries
P.O. Box 3565. Newark, NJ 07103
E-mail: dotgomin@yahoo.com


Cover Illustration by: Tanvir Haider
E-mail:tan.haider@gmail.com
website: http://www.mayamax.com

What do you believe?
Man's paradigms or God's paradigms?

God forbid: yea, let God be true, but every man a liar; as it is written, that thou mightest be justified in thy sayings, and mightest overcome when thou art judged. (Romans 3:4)

# Table of Contents

*INTRODUCTION*                                                     *xiii*

    **Is there hope for a lasting marriage?**              xiv

*Chapter One*                                                          *1*

    **The Divine Purpose of Marriage**                        1

        The Burning Desire for Relationship          2

        Marriage and Spiritual Fellowship            5

        Sex Unites Two People Spiritually            6

        Divorce Rates among Christian Groups          9

        What Has Religion Got to Do with It?         10

        Marriage and Family Scandinavian Style       11

        The State as the Great "Neutraqualizer"      13

        The Impact on the Children                   13

        Where Is God?                                14

        Cohabitation before Marriage is Risky        16

*Chapter Two*                                                        *19*

    **Your Divine Nature vs. Your Dust Nature**             19

        The Devil is After Your Crown                21

        Our Survival Instincts                       23

        Our Sexuality                                24

        "It's a Man's World"                         24

        The Search for Love                          25

        Four Kinds of Love                           26

        Self-aggrandizement                          31

        The Sin of Pride Begins With "I Will"        32

        How Do We Rise Above Pride?                  35

*Chapter Three*                                                      *39*

**Origins of Illicit Spiritual Unions**                              **39**

    Sexuality and the Desires of Demons          41

    Demons Work in Clusters                       42

    Spirit of Jealousy                            43

    Spirit of Heaviness                           44

    Ancestral Covenants and our Stolen Blessings  47

    Evil Family Inheritance                       49

*Chapter Four*                                                       *52*

**Honor God with Your Body**                                         **52**

    Your Body is for God, Your Maker              54

    Indecent Proposal                             56

    Sexual Revolution of the 1960s                58

    Don't Violate Spiritual Laws Concerning Sexuality  60

    Sexual Immorality and Demonic Infestations    62

    No One is Immune from Demonic Attack           63

    Avoid Spiritual Quick Fixes                   64

    Solomon's Delight                             66

    Are People Born with Sexual Aberration?       68

    Help Me! I'm Becoming Transgendered           69

    The Androphile Project                        71

    Teach the Children Sexual Purity              74

    Demons of Peer Pressure                       78

    The Snare of Pornography                      80

    Individual vs. Community Rights               83

    Sexual Uncleanliness                          87

    Sexual Healing: Spiritual Detox               89

*Chapter Five*        *94*

**Spiritual Marriage with a Curse**        **94**

Ancestral Spiritual Marriages and Curses    95

Be Careful of Your "Sweet Nothings"    97

My Funny Valentine with a Curse    98

Evil Spiritual Ruler    98

A Man's Enemies Are within His Own Family    101

The Mother-in-Law vs. Daughter-in-Law Syndrome    102

Delayed or Denied Marriages    103

Dreams as Sources of Spiritual Bondage    105

Evil Deposits    106

The Word of God is Fire    107

Barrenness    108

Satan's Evil Counterfeits    110

Demonic Marks and Signs    111

Beware of Gifts, Jewelry, and Flea Market Bargains    112

Evil behind the Mask    113

Spiritual Mind and Soul Ties    114

God's Power is Available to You    115

*Chapter Six*        *119*

**Marital Anomalies and Counseling**        **119**

The Garden Called Marriage    120

Are We Wired to Cheat?    124

Triangular Love and Child Discipline    128

Benjamin McLane Spock (The Book Says!)    130

Behavioral Science and Spirituality    134

Fatal Attraction    140

The Alpha Male    143

Gentlemen, Our Manhood is under Spiritual Attack    145

Every Home Needs a Father Figure    148

Avoid Verbal Jabs and Demon Talk     152

Honor Thy Father and Mother     155

Separation and Divorce     159

The Effects of Divorce on Kids     160

The Stepchild Syndrome     161

The Good News     162

*Chapter Seven*     *165*

**Rebuilding Relationships**     **165**

The What, How, Why, and Who     168

Always Spiritualize     170

Don't Victimize Your Spouse     175

Love Covers a Multitude of Sins     177

To Forgive, or Not to Forgive?     180

*AppendixPower Prayers*     *185*

**Power Prayers ForMarriage & FamilyRestoration**     187

**References**     **202**

# Prayer for Spiritual Wisdom

*[For I always pray to] the God of our Lord Jesus Christ, the Father of glory, that He may grant you a spirit of wisdom and revelation [of insight into mysteries and secrets] in the [deep and intimate] knowledge of Him,*

*By having the eyes of your heart flooded with light, so that you can know and understand the hope to which He has called you, and how rich is His glorious inheritance in the saints (His set-apart ones),*

*And [so that you can know and understand] what is the immeasurable and unlimited and surpassing greatness of His power in and for us who believe, as demonstrated in the working of His mighty strength,*

*Which He exerted in Christ when He raised Him from the dead and seated Him at His [own] right hand in the heavenly [places],*

*Far above all rule and authority and power and dominion and every name that is named [above every title that can be conferred], not only in this age and in this world, but also in the age and the world which are to come.* *(Ephesians 1:17-21 AMP)*

# INTRODUCTION

## Spiritual Marriage: The Source of hidden problems

As I was working on the book, *"Killing Me Softly"* based on John 10:10, it dawned on me that most of my friends were going through marital problems, with some of them ending in divorce. The first thing that came to mind was how come these couples met and fell in love, but ended up becoming bitter enemies? When you hear about the divorce statistics, you tend to ignore them until it hits too close to home. Even, men, and servants of God have not been spared this catastrophe. Divorce among the clergy is reported to be increasing faster than any other profession. The Lord laid it upon my heart to further explore what is behind these devastations we see in today's broken homes.

This book takes a look at family and marriage institutions from a spiritual perspective with regard to our sexuality and relationship with God, other spiritual entities, and with one another as we approach the end of the age.

We live in a culture where the sanctity of family life in general, and the marriage institution in particular, has come under tremendous attacks. The divorce statistics, and the current decadence of our nation's moral fiber certainly bare this out. Marriages have fallen on the rocks, pushing the family structure into a tailspin.

# Is there hope for a lasting marriage?

Who or what is responsible for the havoc that has been unleashed on the family and marriage? Social scientists have come up with plausible causes and have reached conclusions, based on human observation and research extrapolated from nature, to support their views and findings.

However, in all their deliberations, they have left out the one factor that has been documented and proven to be true throughout the ages and across all cultural lines: that man is part physical, part spiritual. Whenever disaster or tragedy strikes, we tend to invoke the help of the spiritual. But on all other occasions, the spiritual is frowned upon. There is no doubt that a force much larger than ourselves brought the universe into existence and is holding it all together, controlling, and impacting the affairs of men.

A flight attendant once asked me, "How come lions can attack and destroy other lions to get what they want, but when human beings do it, it's considered wrong?" My answer was that human beings were created in the image of our Maker, and He has endowed each one of us with the capacity to refrain from behaving like animals. Our divine nature keeps our animal instincts in check. Certainly, human beings do bad things, even some things that the animal kingdom would never consider doing.

When God created the universe, everything was perfect. Man was placed in paradise. But Adam and Eve listened to the devil and disobeyed God's directive not to eat from the tree of the knowledge of good and evil. When they ate of the forbidden fruit, two types of seeds, good and evil, were imprinted on their psyche. Humans now carry the genes of good and evil. Which of these seeds bear fruit depends on what seed is sown in one's life. You will reap what you sow, whether good or bad. The good seed leads to life; the bad to corruption or sin, and sin to sorrow, and death.

The next logical question then is, "What constitutes good, or evil?"

Who sets the standards? Whose word is truth, and is there such a thing as absolute truth? These are important questions to consider when it comes to issues concerning life in general, and spirituality in particular.

One of the devil's offensive tactics is to destroy the family structure, starting with the marriage institution. To do this, he has attacked our sexuality, spiritually and physically. Why sexuality? Our sexuality is intrinsic, and is at the heart of all our relationships, among fellow human beings and with God. In the past, covenants with spiritual entities to protect the family resulted in a situation where they took advantage and ravished the family. The impact of these spirits were felt, and passed down along generational lines in the form of broken homes, such as separation and divorce, rebellious children and shattered dreams, addictions, and chronic health problems.

To the women, spiritual marriages to demonic entities from your ancestral background are often a source of hidden problems in your relations with men, or your ability to bear children. However, there is a saying that *"You cannot prevent a bird from flying over your head, but you can prevent it from perching there."* Learn to arm all areas of spiritual vulnerabilities in your life.

The big question, though, is how to get people to apply spiritual principles and truths when their spiritual reality has been distorted. Spiritual ignorance, or sloppiness is no excuse. No wonder God laments in Hosea 4:6 that His people are perishing for lack of (spiritual) knowledge. Many in the churches today have excellent knowledge of the Scriptures, and yet are poor in the application of the spiritual principles that are within them. Many are spiritually impotent and impoverished because they have failed to turn doctrine into life experiences.

The devil is not afraid when the Word of Christ is preached. What he fears most is when we obey and subject ourselves to the authority of Christ. Jesus questions, "Why do you call Me, Lord, Lord, and do not [practice] what I tell you?" (Luke 6:46 AMP.) Your spiritual growth or power is determined by your obedience to the teachings of Jesus, and by yielding to the Holy Spirit. Any complacency or disregard to the above directives is tantamount to spiritual suicide.

Later, we will explore why and how evil spirits have overpowered, and married people in the realm of the spirit, contrary to the divine purpose of marriage, to rule and interfere with their lives. It is our responsibility to sever and annul all ties with any demonic third parties to our relationships.

May the Lord Jesus Christ grant us His peace, and may He use this book to strengthen our fellowship with Him and our dealings with one another.

# Chapter One

## The Divine Purpose of Marriage

*Haven't you read, he replied, "that at the beginning the Creator 'made them male and female,' and said, 'For this reason a man will leave his father and mother and be united to his wife, and the two will become one flesh'? So they are no longer two, but one. Therefore what God has joined together, let man not separate."*

*(Matthew 19:4-5 NIV)*

*Let marriage be held in honor (esteemed worthy, precious, of great price, and especially dear) in all things. And thus let the marriage bed be undefiled (kept undishonored); for God will judge and punish the unchaste [all guilty of sexual vice] and adulterous.*

*(Hebrews 13:4 AMP)*

The following is a quote by a lady who shared her views on marriage with Dennis Rainey.

> It's as though I'm scanning a desert with a pair of binoculars. Everywhere I look I see bodies strewn about in various stages of death and dying--divorce, isolation, abusive and decayed relationships, all types of devastation. After viewing this I ask myself, why would I want to begin that journey?
>
> (www.everystudent.com. Is there hope for a lasting Marriage?)

1

# The Burning Desire for Relationship

Our Creator has imprinted on our psyche a deep-seated desire for fellowship and intimacy. When God created man, He did not want him to be alone, and therefore, the Lord God said:

> It is not good (sufficient, satisfactory) that the man should be alone; I will make him a helper meet (suitable, adapted, complementary) for him. (Genesis 2:18 AMP)

In the Garden of Eden, when his partner was presented to him, Adam welcomed the news with joy and gladness.

> And Adam said, This is now bone of my bones, and flesh of my flesh: she shall be called Woman, because she was taken out of Man. (Genesis 2:23)

When paradise was lost due to the sin of disobedience, God proclaimed to the man and woman:

> In the sweat of your face shall you eat bread until you return to the ground, for out of it you were taken; for dust you are and to dust you shall return. (Genesis 3:19 AMP)

> To the woman He said, I will greatly multiply your grief and your suffering in pregnancy and the pangs of childbearing; with spasms of distress you will bring forth children. Yet your desire and craving will be for your husband, and he will rule over you. (Genesis 3:16 AMP)

God designed the marriage institution as a partnership, where the man, although is the head of the household, loves his wife as himself, and where the woman *"respects her husband" (Ephesians 5:33.)* But the relationship became cancerous. Men and women started to devour one another. For example, when a man believes that the woman wants to dominate the relationship or control him, he begins to protect his turf by being abusive. The woman is seen as a nagger. But for a woman to truly fulfill her role as man's helper or partner, she needs to be in the loop of what is happening in her man's life, in order to contribute and improve the relationship. Sometimes this is construed in the wrong way, and the man ends up spurning her love. How does a woman cope or survive in a relationship when one of the most fundamental expressions of her love for her man is seen as a threat? Competition, and the blame game are disparaging in any relationship. Couples should learn how to accommodate, adapt, adjust, and respect what both bring to the marriage. God created woman from the rib (side) of man and not his foot (Genesis 2:22) as society would have us believe.

In the case of battered women, there are societal factors that have reinforced the stereotypical subservient nature of the woman to the man in a relationship. Three of the most blatant views are as follows: The woman is seen as the weaker sex, as a man's property, and as a sex object. Moreover, over the centuries, women have also exploited their sexuality to their advantage or to their disadvantage as the case may be. Ayanna succinctly illustrates these points in an article "The Exploitation of Women in Hip-hop Culture" that said, "Many women [have] defined their own worth on what they can do for and get from a man. Some women were willing to take risks with their bodies, minds and hearts hoping to raise their socio-economic status and gain security for their children's future, and they have learned to use their sexuality to do this." *(The Exploitation of Women in Hip-hop Culture-My Sistahs. © 2001, Advocates for Youth).*

Any abusive relationship is physically and spiritually demoralizing, making the woman feel that her life is hopeless and worthless. If this is true, how and why does a woman stay in an abusive relationship? Social scientists are equally baffled. And according to Bessel van der Kolk, MD, professor of psychiatry at Boston University Medical School, one of the hardest tasks for mental health professionals is to "re-wire" people, especially women, and free them from the cycle of abusive relationships. *"Paradoxically, these people get pulled back to dangerous and abusive situations."* In 2005, the story of country singer Mindy McCready who became pregnant, by her ex-boyfriend after he had been charged with her attempted murder a couple of months earlier, is a case similar in point. Why this anomaly?

Clinical psychologists say when a person is repeatedly traumatized, the brain secretes biochemical endogenous hormones that can deaden the senses and put the body into survival mode to cope with physical abuse and adjust to the reality of the relationship. In this way, some women become conditioned to take the abuse. Very insightful!

The true reason why a woman is not able to leave right away is because spiritually and subconsciously, her desire is for her man, to stay by his side, to help him as mandated by God. The world does not understand this and calls the woman a victim who does not love herself. When the man has fallen, who else is there to lift him up but the woman, his other half? In Ecclesiastes we read:

> Two are better than one; because they have a good reward for their labour. For if they fall, the one will lift up his fellow: but woe to him that is alone when he falleth; for he hath not another to help him up. Again, if two lie together, then they have heat: but how can one be warm alone? And if one prevail against him, two shall withstand him; and a threefold cord is not quickly broken. (Ecclesiastes 4:9-12)

A marriage relationship in which God is a third party to the union cannot easily be broken. Today, you hear from all the talk shows that a woman must be out of her mind if she verbalizes her intention to try to salvage her marriage. If she expresses any hope for the relationship, and tries to work out her problems, she is told she is in denial. She is in denial of what, for wanting to save her marriage and keep the family together? In fact, what these people are advocating is for the woman to renege on her vows and to express her "animal instinct," the part of her that says, "I come first."

In the past, most of the women who said they would kick out a cheating partner found that it was easier said than done. Why? Spiritually, there is more to a marriage relationship than meets the eye. A person who is wise always seeks help, but the unspiritual refuses help and his home catches fire.

Some women see marriage as idiosyncratic, so when they weigh the pluses and minuses, with regard to the many devastations happening to relationships in the rest of society, they become philosophical. They give their men the benefit of the doubt, believing that they are doing the best they can. Eventually, some women are able to break away from these abusive marriages. But for those who decide to stick with the marriage, psychotherapists insist that the cheating partner must make a real effort to change. They insist that the cheating partner give candid answers to questions about the affair, like "who, why, where, do you still love her, and is it over?" But what these counselors don't realize is that it is hard finding peace in a marriage or a relationship, especially if the problems are spiritually induced or where demonic spiritual third parties are involved in the union or partnership.

Throughout this book, we will explore how third-party spiritual entities have forced their way into many relationships, causing most of the devastations we see in today's families and broken homes.

## Marriage and Spiritual Fellowship

There are many references in the Bible describing our union with God like a marital union (see Ezekiel 16:7-8). God designed the family bond as a way to develop not only physical intimacy here on earth, but also as a precursor to our spiritual intimacy and fellowship with Him through our Lord Jesus Christ in heaven.

> Then I saw a new heaven and a new earth, for the first heaven and the first earth had passed away, and there was no longer any sea.
>
> I saw the Holy City, the new Jerusalem, coming down out of heaven from God, prepared as a bride beautifully dressed for her husband.
>
> And I heard a loud voice from the throne saying, "Now the dwelling of God is with men, and he will live with them. They will be his people, and God himself will be with them and be their God." (Revelation 21:1-3 NIV)

In marriage, an intimate bond is developed. Children are born, loved, raised, and nurtured with a sense of belonging and fellowship. With God in your marriage, the spiritual covering for the family is strong, and the husband and wife are in one accord. The covering acts as a shield or barrier for the family, against all intruders to your relationship.

God values marital relationships. He will therefore not hold you guiltless if you cheapen sex, or denigrate or mock marriage as instituted by Him. Marriage is between male and female. God does not endorse counterfeit marriages and other living arrangements.

## Sex Unites Two People Spiritually

It is no accident that we have marriage ceremonies such as engagements, wedding, and so forth. The symbolisms and rites attached to the marriage union have spiritual implications. In God's eyes, sex in marriage unites and binds a man and a woman in a spiritual covenant, as one. This covenant is activated when vows are exchanged and the union consummated in sexual intercourse. The release of virgin blood when a woman's hymen is broken presupposes sexual purity to the covenant. Virgin blood is symbolic of the divine blood our Savior Jesus, the Christ shed at Calvary, consummating His union with His people in an everlasting covenant.

Sex in marriage is indeed full of spiritual mysteries, and the devil seeks to distort and destroy our relationships by exploiting our ignorance.

We live in a world where we seem to disrespect sexual boundaries. Many are ignorant of the spiritual laws that govern sexuality in general, and sex within the marriage institution in particular, as designed and ordained by the Lord God Almighty, Creator of heaven and earth. Sex, is as much a spiritual union as body contact or physical romance. As written in Scripture, "The two shall become one flesh" (Genesis 2:24).

Sex is sacred. Through sex, we consummate our marital vows before God, with men as witnesses to the covenant. Since a marital vow is a sacred covenant, God will judge any casual or illicit sex, according to Hebrews 13:4 which says, "Marriage should be honored by all, and the marriage bed kept pure, for God will judge the adulterer and all the sexually immoral."

Therefore be careful to honor marriage, and guard the sacredness of sexual intimacy between wife and husband. In Proverbs God exhorts us as follows:

> Let your fountain [of human life] be blessed [with the rewards of fidelity], and rejoice in the wife of your youth.
> (Proverbs 5:18 AMP)

God has very good reasons for wanting you to enjoy your spouse in a monogamous relationship. When you make a sacred vow before Him, He honors that vow. God respects sex between man and wife to the extent that we are not to deprive each other of sex, except by mutual consent:

> Defraud ye not one the other, except it be with consent for a time, that ye may give yourselves to fasting and prayer; and come together again, that Satan tempt you not for your incontinency *[lack of restraint of sexual desire]*
> (1 Corinthians 7:5 *Comments added*)

Any violation of the above directives, any infidelity or disrespect for your mate becomes a stumbling block to your spiritual life. God will not even listen to your prayers and petitions. In Malachi we read:

> Here is another thing you do. You cover the LORD's altar with tears, weeping and groaning because he pays no attention to your offerings, and he doesn't accept them with pleasure.
>
> You cry out, "Why has the LORD abandoned us?" I'll tell you why! Because the LORD witnessed the vows you and your wife made to each other on your wedding day when you were young. But you have been disloyal to her, though she remained your faithful companion, the wife of your marriage vows.
>
> Didn't the LORD make you one with your wife? In body and spirit you are his. And what does he want? Godly children from your union. So guard yourself; remain loyal to the wife of your youth.      (Malachi 2:13-15 NLT)

God wants godly children from your union, not bastards. In the Old Testament, any disobedience in this directive resulting in an out-of-wedlock child was grounds for the child to be excluded from the congregation of the Lord for ten generations.

> A bastard shall not enter into the congregation of the LORD; even to his tenth generation shall he not enter into the congregation of the LORD.    (Deuteronomy 23:2)

Any curse operating in your life must be nullified. Thank God, Jesus died on the cross and became a curse for His followers.

> Christ hath redeemed us from the curse of the law, being made a curse for us: for it is written, Cursed is every one that hangeth on a tree.    (Galatians 3:13)

If you are a Christian and you fall into the above category, by faith invoke and plead the blood of Jesus. Declare and decree to nullify the curse, ten generations back on either side of your parents.

Sexual sins carry spiritual and physical ramifications. In the Bible, God makes numerous references to avoid illicit sexual encounters. The seventh and the tenth of the Ten Commandments forbid adultery. There are repercussions for violating your marriage vows or cheating on your spouse. Moses warned the Israelites:

> If you make a vow to the LORD your God, do not be slow to pay it, for the LORD your God will certainly demand it of you and you will be guilty of sin.    (Deuteronomy 23:21 NIV)

Don't let the devil deceive you through the so-called sex experts, and therapists who counsel you, contrary to the Word of God, to follow youthful, lustful fantasies in order to discover your "true" sexual identity. Don't be taken in by worldly philosophies and wisdom to gratify your sensuality.

The lust of the eyes and flesh, the pride of life, selfishness, greediness, lying, judgmentalism, impatience, unforgiveness, blasphemy, and lack of spirituality, all lead to nothing but trouble, sorrow, and death of relationships.

# Divorce Rates among Christian Groups

The devil is making his presence felt in Christian homes. In 1999, a survey conducted by the Barna Research Group in Ventura, California, found that 29 percent of all adult Baptists had been through a divorce. Among Christian groups, only those who attend non-denominational Protestant churches were more likely to be divorced, with a 34 percent divorce rate.

A break-down along racial lines revealed that whites were more likely to have had a divorce, at 27 percent, than African-Americans (22 percent), Hispanics (20 percent), and Asians (8 percent). Conservative Protestant Christians, on average, had the highest divorce rate, as opposed to a much lower rate by mainline Christians. Atheists and agnostics had the lowest divorce rate. *(US Divorce rate: Religious Tolerance Group)*

The above statistics have cast severe doubt on the ability of religion, particularly the Christian faith, to safeguard the sanctity of marriage. In search for answers, some have pointed to the lack of communication skills as the culprit. According to Hughes:

> In the churches, people have a superstitious view that Christianity will keep them from divorce, but they are subject to the same problems as everyone else, and they include a lack of relationship skills. ...Just being born again is not a rabbit's foot. *(Donald Hughes, author of The Divorce Reality).*

Hughes further maintained that 90 percent of divorces among born-again couples occur after they have been "saved." So many believe religion can do little or nothing to stop the decay and devastations we see in our relationships.

Marriage is a divine institution, and it is currently under spiritual attack. No section of society is immune. Religion alone is not enough.

Just as faith without works is dead, religion without spirituality is of no value to God, or mankind.

# What Has Religion Got to Do with It?

An *Associate Press* article by David Crary revealed that no state in the Bible belt was more affected by the divorce problem than Oklahoma, where Governor Frank Keating enlisted clergymen, academics, lawyers and psychologists in a campaign to reduce the divorce rate by a third by 2009. *(David Crary, "Bible Belt Leads U.S. in Divorces.")*

## Variation in divorce rates by religion

| Religion | % have been divorced |
|---|---|
| Jews | 30% |
| Born-again Christians | 27% |
| Other Christians | 24% |
| Atheists, Agnostics | 21% |

Source: Religious Tolerance Group 10/21/2004

## Variation in divorce rates among Christian faith groups

| Denomination in order of decreasing divorce rate | % who have been divorce |
|---|---|
| Non-denominational (small groups; independents) | 34% |
| Baptists | 29% |
| Mainline Protestants | 25% |
| Mormons | 24% |
| Catholics | 21% |
| Lutherans | 21% |

Source: Religious Tolerance Group10/21/2004

The above findings seem to fly in the face of the slogan "The family that prays together stays together." After all, aren't Christians supposed to follow biblical principles indicative of sound teachings, protective of marriage and the family bond, which the secular world so craves? The data seems to undermine the notion that the church is providing practical and life-changing values in support of marriages.

Does this data point to the ineffectiveness of how churches minister to families? Or is there a wider sinister plot to undermine the family structure and the marriage institution that the church cannot handle? Considering the apparently lower divorce rate among atheists, and agnostics, it is not surprising that some researchers have suggested that religion may have little or no effect on divorce rates, but that other factors such as education and/or finances may have a greater influence. But we must not discount the influences of the powerful spiritual realm. This brings up the question of the differences between religion and spirituality.

Religion is the institutionalized doctrine of one's beliefs. The atheist and the agnostic both have a religion: it is the choice not to believe in or recognize the impact of a higher divinity on their lives. The unspiritual does not believe that there are spiritual forces behind every societal vice and problems in our lives.

Spirituality, on the other hand, is how you interpret and practice your beliefs. Religion without spirituality is useless. As a result, in today's churches, people have become spiritually impotent, incapable of detecting the insidiousness of the devil's tactics of stealing, killing, and destroying the blessings in their lives. Those who understand spiritual warfare know that there are evil forces behind every troubled marriage. The devil is behind every societal trend that attempts to discredit and undermine holy matrimony as instituted by God. The resultant rise in children born out of wedlock and the divorce rate dishonor the marriage and family institution, and is an affront to God.

## Marriage and Family Scandinavian Style

An article appeared in *USA TODAY* titled *"Nordic Family ties don't mean tying the knot."* It gives us a glimpse of what is happening to marriage and family life in the Scandinavian countries (Norway, Sweden, and Denmark). Nowhere in the western hemisphere is the assault on marriage and family more prominent than in Scandinavia. The attempt to redress some women issues, and make them competitive with the men, have ushered in a situation where the direct linkage between marriage and having children means nothing to many people. It has become common for couples to live together and have children without marriage. According to the article, Scandinavians who don't marry tend to fall into one of two categories: those who believe the traditional same-father/same-mother family model is largely outmoded, and those who think it is too big of a commitment than parenting.

People who think that marriage is meaningless also miss out on its spiritual significance for the overall well-being of their families. Meanwhile, Satan, the god of this world, blinds them into thinking they are masters of their own destinies. Eventually, all sexual and sensual boundaries are tested, or pushed aside as antiquated. From the Bible, we learn that during the end times the spiritual powers that ruled ancient Egyptian and later Babylonian kingdoms would once again rule the earth. References can be found in Revelation 14:8, Daniel 4:30, Isaiah 21:9, and Jeremiah 51:7 to mention a few.

The peculiarities of these kingdoms include lust, sensual living, idolatry (anything you give supreme devotion to other than God), unholy desires, greed, sexual promiscuity, fornication, adultery, abortions, infanticide, homosexuality, incest, pornography, sexual abuse, divorce, and spiritual uncleanliness such as witchcraft.

These end time spirits would use women as mediums and raise them to positions of power just as they did with the cult of Ashtoreth in ancient Babylon. These women become the head of families, the high priest of the home instead of their men or husbands with a far-reaching impact for societies.

In the US, about two-thirds of all divorces are initiated by women. (*Popenoe, David,* Debunking the Divorce Myths Copyright 2002. The National Marriage Project at Rutgers University, New Brunswick.) The court system even blindly favors women in custody battles.

# The State as the Great "Neutraqualizer"

To the Nordics, the separation of church and state meant that there was little pressure for people to get married based on religious beliefs. In an effort to cater to societal trends that promoted equality for women, the government took a laissez-faire attitude not to interfere with how people lived their lives or raised their children. The government became a neutralizing force when it enacted laws and policies designed to help make family life easier for single mothers. Although there are divisions for children and family affairs, they exist not to promote family values, but to facilitate amicable family breakups and to safeguard the interests of single mothers and their children. The Scandinavian governments have also supported family policies economically. About two-thirds of single mothers in Sweden receive housing allowances. In addition, the state provides children with maintenance allowances, in case deadbeat dads don't pay child support. To top it all, family leave in Scandinavia is reported to range from one to two years, with 80 percent pay.

In the United Nations' quality-of-life survey for 2004, which rates per-capital income, education levels, health care, and life expectancy in measuring a nation's well-being, Norway ranked first and Sweden second. The USA came in eighth according to the *USA TODAY* article.

# The Impact on the Children

Social attitudes toward equality have impacted marriage traditions in a subtle profound way. According to the above article, "Traditional households headed by male wage earners have waned, giving way to everything from single-parent households to families that combine the children that parents have had together, and with other partners" in a "his, mine, and ours" chop suey.

There are some who worry about the negative impact these relationships have on children. As the children get older, some do not see the importance of a biological father for their children.

Although a child is a man's seed, some women see the children as their own. One woman put it, "You choose a father and then you choose a different husband."

In the end, these young people decide what they feel is in their best interest, and not any antiquated beliefs of their uneducated female ancestors. Besides, with the state as a great "Neutraqualizer," on their side, any belief in God that restricts or encroaches on their newfound liberation is an affront to them.

In America, the percentage of out-of-wedlock children has more than tripled since 1970, according to the article. It goes on to point out that on both sides of the Atlantic, two of the three forces that have driven up the birth rate for unmarried mothers are feminism and the decline of religion. One young lady, who summed up the current view of holy matrimony compared to generations ago, is reported to have said: "It would be blasphemous for her to get married in a church. A civil service would be 'highly unromantic' and a lot of papers to fill in and ceremony to go through for something that might not really last that long, because you never know."

The idea of the marriage as a sacred commitment is ludicrous to some people, given the current reality of bad marriages. Over their lifetime, these children have seen the enormous devastation of broken marriages on families. Why should they risk their happiness on the command of a "helpless" God, if in fact there is a God?

## Where Is God?

To even mention religion as a stabilizing force is a turn-off. In the article one woman was quoted as saying, "Every single war, every single conflict, everything has been based on religion; so it just reaches a point where you say, 'If God is that great, he's not doing a very good job, is he?' Eventually, you end up choosing not to believe because to me it's just too much of a contradiction. I've got to hope there's no God, because if there is, I've got some issues with him." This is well said, but who is to be blamed, God, the government, or society? To me, the onus is on a society that forgot, or neglected to teach children moral absolutes in favor of self-indulgence, right over wrong, the holy versus the profane.

People make choices, and God respects the decisions they make. The government does not dictate to whom people should be given in marriage. Society, on the other hand, gives you options, but it is up to you to decide what you think is right and wrong, vis-à-vis what you believe would make you happy.

For example, whereas in America, the father gives the bride away in marriage, in Sweden the bride walks down the aisle alone. When societal trend reaches a point, where the groom no longer asks for permission from the parents of his future bride, from whom do you seek help when the marriage hits a snag? Why blame God when you disobey His laws and want Him out of your life, when you dishonor your parents, when you neglect the spiritual, and so in your ignorance you fall prey to the forces of evil, which currently sets standards, and trends for this world?

Have you ever considered how spiritual principalities and powers influence the trend of the world? Ideas become a way of life. Things become trendy and everybody gets into the act both young and old. In often times, these are contrary to the word of God. In Revelations we read of the fate of *Babylon the Great*, a worldwide spiritual power, the mother of harlots and abominations of the earth (Revelation 17:5), which has interfered in the affairs of men. She has superimposed her rulership on all the earth as revealed by the angel to John: *"The waters you saw, where the prostitute sits, are peoples, multitudes, nations and languages" (Revelation 17:15 NIV)*. Unholy, prostitution does not only means sexual decadence, but also selling ourselves to the counterfeit things of the devil instead of God.

America was founded on Judeo-Christian principles, and therefore family values are important. Whenever there is an upward trend in family crisis, the nation is put on alert. There are soul-searching and social dialogues for ways to deal with the issue. But not so with the

Nordics! What then does the average Scandinavian think about the American family? According to the article, the Nordics "tend to see American views on marriage and children as conservative at best, and hypocritical at worst, pointing out the high divorce rates in the USA."

## Cohabitation before Marriage is Risky

With the alarming rate of divorce in America, it is not surprising that a growing percentage of committed couples have decided to live common law rather than getting married. The record number of babies born out of wedlock supports the prevalence of cohabitation in this country. An *Associated Press* article titled, "More unmarried women having children" quoted government reports that showed nearly 1.5 million babies were born to unmarried women in 2004.

According to the National Center for Health Statistics (NCHS.), this accounted for 35.7 percent of all births in the USA. Of this figure, teens accounted for only one-quarter of the births to single women. Even for those who plan to marry, cohabitation has become a tempting option. But these relationships frequently do not last because God does not endorse, nor will He bless premarital living arrangements.

In a report *"Cohabitation before Marriage: High Divorce Rate,"* Dr. Dave and Dr. Dee reported:

> The divorce rate in the United States is high, with estimates anywhere from 40% to 60%. However, divorce rates are even higher for those who cohabitate before marriage. About 40% of cohabitants break up before getting married. But of those who do get married, the divorce rate is nearly 50% higher for cohabitants than for non-cohabitants. The evidence seems to show that living together before marriage increases the risk of divorce. (http://www.drdaveanddee.com/cohabitation)

In time past, when young adults started dating each other, the expectation was to get married and have the same spouse for their entire lives. Given the current reality of the divorce rate in America, are these expectations an illusion? Not at all! Our Creator has endowed in each of us the inalienable right to a life partner and to enjoy that union to the exclusion of all others. However, marriage does not come easy or cheap. Despite the blessings in marriage, Paul warned us of the cost and challenges inherent in the marriage union, when he wrote:

> But if you do marry, you do not sin [in doing so], and if a virgin marries, she does not sin [in doing so]. Yet those who marry will have physical and earthly troubles, and I would like to spare you that.     (1 Corinthians 7:28 AMP)

You have to work at your marriage relationships. Be careful though, there are always spiritual forces determined to ruin them. You must remain spiritually vigilant. Be careful of your priorities, because you will reap what you sow. Invest in people instead of things, for bigger rewards here on earth, and an eternal treasure in heaven.

Those who put careers ahead at the cost of marriage and family relationships, eventually become losers spiritually. When you lose your family, a part of you is also lost. Blood is thicker than water. Spiritual bond is stronger than physical bond, so children, despite the love of their adopted parents, still seek after their biological parents because of the spiritual bond. The truth of the matter is that spiritual relationships among people whether good or evil are always stronger no matter how the spiritual union was established. The family and marriage institutions are very important to God, and so He rewards those who care and obey His precepts. According to the psalmist:

> BLESSED (HAPPY, fortunate, to be envied) is everyone who fears, reveres, and worships the Lord, who walks in His ways and lives according to His commandments.
> For you shall eat [the fruit] of the labor of your hands; happy (blessed, fortunate, enviable) shall you be, and it shall be well with you.
>
> Your wife shall be like a fruitful vine in the innermost parts of your house; your children shall be like olive plants round about your table.

God's promises come with conditions. These promises far outweigh the conditions and yet we always fail to see the benefits meant for our good. What prevents us from obeying God to do the right things? What is within us that makes us susceptible to making wrong choices? The true answer can be found the in the realm of the spirit.

In the next chapter, we will explore the fallen state of man, how the devil tempts and uses our dust nature to alienate us from God, to undermine among other things, the family structure, the marriage institution, and our relationships with one another.

# Chapter Two

## Your Divine Nature vs. Your Dust Nature

*Then the Lord God formed man from the dust of the ground and breathed into his nostrils the breath or spirit of life, and man became a living being.* *(Genesis 2:7 AMP)*

Man is a mixture of dust and divine breath. Our dust nature is in cahoots with our sinful nature to gratify the desires of the flesh, which include (1) our survival instincts, (2) our sexuality and its passions, and (3) our desire to be somebody "Self," (the center of our flesh). The key is for Self to be under the control of God's Spirit.

Our divine nature, on the other hand, is said to consist of (1) our dignity (the God breath in us), (2) our God-given dominion of the earth, and (3) our destiny or crown, which is our God-given free-will power. The key here is for our free-will to submit to God's authority.

One of the main methodologies of the devil is temptation, and that has not changed since the Garden of Eden. The devil is constantly looking for ways, and opportunities to lure us into breaking God's commandments. In the Garden the lie was:

> You will not surely die, for God knows that when you eat of it
> your eyes will be opened, and you will be like God, knowing
> good and evil. When the woman [the weaker sex; *in this day
> and age it could be the man*] saw that the fruit of the tree was
> good for food and pleasing to the eye (lust), and desirable for
> gaining wisdom (self-aggrandizement), she took some and ate
> it. She also gave some to her husband, who was with her, and he
> ate it.                                  (Genesis 3:4-6 AMP *comments added*)

Our archenemy, the devil, tempts us in the two main areas of our being or personality. One is through our divine nature, and the other through our dust nature (our survival or "animal" instincts).

In the wilderness, the devil tempted Jesus, saying, "If you're the Son of God (tempting the divine nature with pride), tell these stones to become bread." After forty days who would not want to eat? The devil tempts our dust nature, our survival instincts as it were, with food. The devil also entices Self to indulge in our sensuality.

The second temptation in the wilderness was similar. "If you are the Son of God, throw yourself down." All temptations are to elevate Self above God's laws. The devil goes on to quote the Scriptures:

> He will command his angels concerning you, and they will
> lift you up in their hands, so that you will not strike your foot
> against a stone.                                (Matthew 4:6)

Jesus' answer to the devil was, "Do not put the Lord your God to the test" (Matthew 4:7). Jesus quoted from Deuteronomy 6:16. You have to fight fire with fire, spirit with spirit. Always compare Scripture with Scripture.

My friend, the devil knows the Scriptures more than you may think. He was quoting Psalm 91:11-12. That is why it is so imperative that you study and meditate on the Scriptures so that you do not fall prey to spiritual pride, or succumb to partial truths and mediocrity in your spiritual growth. Ask the Holy Spirit for spiritual discernment and wisdom, and you will not be far from the will of God.

# The Devil is After Your Crown

After creation, God gave dominion of the earth to man. But when Adam and Eve disobeyed God in the Garden, the devil took illegitimate control of the earth. Satan is therefore after your crown, or authority. He is a thief, who has stolen virtually everything he owns but behaves as if it was all his from the beginning. This present world is under his control, until it is destroyed to make room for a new one with no evil or suffering, as it was in the beginning, in paradise.

In one of the three temptations, Satan offered to give Jesus all the kingdoms of this world with its splendor if He would worship him. We read:

> And the devil said unto him, All this power will I give thee, and the glory of them: for that is delivered unto me; and to whomsoever I will I give it. If thou therefore wilt worship me, all shall be thine. And Jesus answered and said unto him, Get thee behind me, Satan: for it is written, Thou shalt worship the Lord thy God, and him only shalt thou serve.     (Luke 4:6-8)

Satan loves to be adored. He did not resist the desire to receive such worship, which rightly belongs to the Creator, as mentioned in Ezekiel 28:12-19. Not only did he try to usurp this worship, he wanted God's throne as well according to Isaiah 14:10-15. Satan, also known as Lucifer, an archangel, was in charge of worship before his fall. Therefore, he knows of the heavenly blessings that have been prepared for our enjoyment. But because of his rebellion, he can no longer partake of this heavenly bliss. We are told:

> For it is impossible for those who were once enlightened, and have tasted of the heavenly gift, and were made partakers of the Holy Ghost, And have tasted the good word of God, and the powers of the world to come, If they shall fall away, to renew them again unto repentance.     (Hebrews 6:4-6)

No wonder he hates man in general, and Christians in particular, because of our divine inheritance, of those who do the will of God. The devil, your enemy, is real and crafty. He is engaged in a spiritual battle, and his passion is to defeat and destroy everything good that God has made. The fight between God, and the devil is also over our crown, our free will to worship God, as it was in paradise. Man was created to worship God and to have intimate relationship with Him. As a child of God, when you worship, and by exchange cast down your crown at the feet of Jesus, God gives you your glory. This mystery has been kept hidden for ages and generations, but is now made manifest to his saints; namely, *"Christ in you, the hope of glory" (Colossians 1:26-27)*. If you don't know Jesus Christ as your personal Savior, you cannot partake of the glory of God. In the gospel of John, Jesus said:

> And the glory which thou gavest me I have given them; that
> they may be one, even as we are one.          (John 17:22)

When you refuse to totally surrender to Jesus, you play into Satan's hand by worshiping your dust nature. You make Self, as a god or an idol (Romans 1:21-23). But God has declared: *"I am the LORD; that is my name! I will not give my glory to another or my praise to idols" (Isaiah 48:2)*. Your old self must be crucified. (Romans 6:6.)

As a Christian, do you know your rights and power over the devil? Jesus, by going to the cross, conquered Satan, and in a way has returned dominion of the earth to us. In Luke, Jesus said:

> I saw Satan falling like a lightning [flash] from heaven. Behold!
> I have given you authority and power to trample upon serpents
> and scorpions, and [physical and mental strength and ability]
> over all the power that the enemy [possesses]; and nothing shall
> in any way harm you.              Luke 10:18-19 AMP)

Although the devil is a defeated foe, he still holds on to the dominion of earth, which he stole from mankind. The devil is a liar, a hater of man, and that has been his nature from the beginning. As Satan, he opposes; as an accuser, he slanders God's people the same way he slandered God to Adam and Eve in the Garden of Eden.

The big question many people ask is, "If God is there, why is there so much suffering in the world?" But my question rather is, "What is it in man that has made him susceptible to evil and suffering?" For the purpose of this book, we will focus on the spiritual causes and their physical manifestations in our lives. First, let's look at the spiritual dynamics of our dust nature, starting with our instincts to survive.

## Our Survival Instincts

One of the three components of our dust nature is our instinct to survive. Our survival instincts deal foremost with our ability to take care of our physical bodies with regard to food, clothing, and shelter. Our drive for prosperity and materialistic tendencies are found here. On the flipside, we also find greediness and selfishness, which are part of the negative, destructive tendencies inherent in our humanity. When our first parents disobeyed God, they incurred His wrath. God decreed that man would toil and sweat in order to eat. God told Adam, our first father:

> Because you listened to your wife and ate from the tree about which I commanded you, 'You must not eat of it,' "Cursed is the ground because of you; through painful toil you will eat of it all the days of your life. It will produce thorns and thistles for you, and you will eat the plants of the field.
>
> By the sweat of your brow you will eat your food until you return to the ground, since from it you were taken; for dust you are and to dust you will return.         (Genesis 3:17-19 NIV)

God has decreed that man must work before he eats. Since money represents the work of our hands, the sweat of our brow, don't withhold wages. Our ambition for fast, easy money could lead to our own undoing according to Proverbs 28:22. The wealth we have accumulated may not engender the happiness we desire; that is why the children of rich parents aren't always the happiest people. Anybody who listens to his spouse to do the wrong thing will bear the consequences. But to those who love God and obey His commandments, He says, "Those who love me inherit wealth, for I fill their treasuries" (Proverbs 8:21 NLT). When God gives you wealth, He does not attach sorrow to it. (Proverbs 10:22.)

## Our Sexuality

Our sexuality is defined first by our gender. God created male and female for a purpose: for humans to multiply and have dominion over the earth. Sexual attraction is part of the Creator's goal to ensure that His divine will is carried out as planned. The chemistry between male and female is embodied in our passions and desires for relationships with one another. On the divine side of our being, intimacy is inflamed by *agape* love. But on our dust side, attraction and intimacy are dictated by erotic infatuation and lust, which are closely tied to our fleshly desire for instant gratification. However, this is contrary to the will of the Holy Spirit for the saints.

Often when people meet someone they feel attracted to, they fail to take inventory of the personalities of their prospective lover because of their lustful desire for instant gratification. When we make a free-will choice, God respects our decision. But the lack of compatibility with our partner is a recipe for disaster. Sooner or later, we realize that our partner is not perfect, forgetting that we ourselves are not perfect. Why expect perfection when we are not perfect?

As a result, the gripe you often hear from the man concerning the woman is *"she doesn't respect me."* If the woman is the breadwinner, her respond is, *"he envies me."* But the male ego is fragile, and cannot stand idle, while the woman usurps his glory.

## "It's a Man's World"

The remark "It's a man's world" has its truism in the fact that God cursed Eve (the woman) as written:

> To the woman He said, I will greatly multiply your grief and your suffering in pregnancy and the pangs of childbearing; with spasms of distress you will bring forth children. Yet your desire and craving will be for your husband, and he will rule over you. (Genesis 3:16 AMP)

Over the years women have been trying to shake off this yoke. Feminism has come a long way, but God has decreed the male to be the head of the family. Does it surprise you why women are not able to easily move away from abusive relationships? Some people believe it has a lot more to do with economics and education than anything else. The assumption here is that no rich, educated woman would be caught in an abusive relationship, reserved only for the uneducated, the poor, perhaps dysfunctional families, if the premises were entirely true.

Spiritually, the man has rule over the woman. He is the crown of her life. So are children (Proverbs. 17:6). Why do you think women always want to marry, and have children? No matter how difficult raising children may be, women still find it rewarding. No matter how ugly a child may appear to be, the spiritual maternal bond makes loving the child possible, thus the saying, "only a mother can love."

It is the ingrained duty or the maternal instinct for the woman to take care of the man's seed, so the rationale from an abused woman is always the children. Of course it is. In fact, it is in the child that the true desire and love of a woman for her man is fulfilled. True love is a spiritual weapon; it gives you the ability to stay together in peace. What is love any way?

## The Search for Love

The English language tends to lump all kinds of "love" into one meaning. The Eskimos have eight ways of defining the word *snow,* which is important to their survival. Nobody wants to mistake an icy snowstorm for snow flurries. This is no different when it comes to love. What is love? How do you define love? Many people don't know or understand true love, and so love, like beauty, is in the eyes of the beholder. Some therefore, mistake lust and infatuation for true spiritual or divine love, which is genuine, and everlasting. True love is a real gem, and only those who have been trained and nurtured by it, ever appreciate its true purpose and value. The unspiritual does not and cannot comprehend divine love.

# Four Kinds of Love

A group of teenagers were asked the question, "What kind of person do you want to marry?" Below is an insightful response given by a seventeen-year-old girl, which reflects today's misunderstanding of love as found in most relationships. This young lady said:

> Marrying someone you're madly in love with is a bad idea--you can't have a good relationship based on something so unstable. I'll marry someone who shares my core values. People who want to marry for love, regardless of similar values, are foolish romantics who will be bitterly disappointed."
> ("I want to marry someone who," *Parade* magazine, 9/14/2003).

In classical Greek literature there are at least four different kinds of words for love.

## *Eros*

*Eros* (Greek, *e'ros*) is passionate love, sexual, erotic, romantic, or sensual desire and longing that one can have for a member of the opposite sex. Eros is an unstable love, closely tied to the flesh, self-indulgence, and greed. In the Bible you are therefore encouraged to:

> Drink waters out of your own cistern [of a pure marriage relationship], and fresh running waters out of your own well. Should your offspring be dispersed abroad as water brooks in the streets? [Confine yourself to your own wife] let your children be for you alone, and not the children of strangers with you.
>
> Let your fountain [of human life] be blessed [with the rewards of fidelity], and rejoice in the wife of your youth.
>
> Let her be as the loving hind and pleasant doe [tender, gentle, attractive]--let her bosom satisfy you at all times, and always be transported with delight in her love.
>
> Why should you, my son, be infatuated with a loose woman, embrace the bosom of an outsider, and go astray?
> (Proverbs 5:15-20 AMP)

# *Phileo*

*Phileo* (Greek, *phi li´a*) is brotherly love among friends. This love grows out of deep personal affection between friends, family, and community, and requires virtue, equality, and familiarity to flourish and nurture.

*Phileo* love is the bond that exists between close friends, similar to the one that existed between David and Jonathan, and between Jesus and Lazarus. In the Bible, we read:

> When David had finished speaking to Saul, the soul of Jonathan was knit with the soul of David, and Jonathan loved him as his own life. (1 Samuel 18:1 AMP)

> So the sisters sent to Him, saying, Lord, he whom You love [so well] is sick. (John 11:3 AMP)

# *Storge*

The Greek word *stor´ge* is maternal bond, the love of parents for a child, or love that grows between family members. A maternal love would ask King Solomon to give her son to the other woman in order to spare his life. Maternal love would fight for the life of her child when the child's husband wants a vegetative spouse to starve to death by disconnecting her feeding tube in the name of dignity.

# *Agape*

The Greek word *aga´pe* love is spiritual or divine love that God sheds in our lives because He is love. The Spirit of God in you produces love. In 1 John we read:

> Whoever does not love does not know God, because God is love. We love because he first loved us. If anyone says, "I love God," yet hates his brother, he is a liar. For anyone who does not love his brother, whom he has seen, cannot love God, whom he has not seen. And he has given us this command: Whoever loves God must also love his brother.
> (1 John 4:8; 19-21 NIV)

> Be imitators of God, therefore, as dearly loved children and
> live a life of love, just as Christ loved us and gave himself up
> for us as a fragrant offering and sacrifice to God.
>
> (Ephesians 5:1-2 NIV)

When a balance is maintained among the four kinds of love, to fulfill
God's command to love one another, marriages tend to last, and
there is harmony in the family. Any inordinate dependence on the
first three is a cause for concern, because they can easily fade or be
corrupted. They are motivated by practical reasons; one or both of
the parties benefit from the relationship. Only *agape* love, or divine
love, is long lasting and not opportunistic or subject to manipulation.
True spiritual love is underscored by the virtues embodied in Paul's
first letter to the Corinthians on love as follows:

> If I [can] speak in the tongues of men and [even] of angels, but
> have not love (that reasoning, intentional, spiritual devotion
> such as is inspired by God's love for and in us), I am only a
> noisy gong or a clanging cymbal.
>
> And if I have prophetic powers (the gift of interpreting
> the divine will and purpose), and understand all the secret
> truths and mysteries and possess all knowledge, and if I have
> [sufficient] faith so that I can remove mountains, but have not
> love (God's love in me) I am nothing (a useless nobody).
>
> Even if I dole out all that I have [to the poor in providing] food,
> and if I surrender my body to be burned or in order that I may
> glory, but have not love (God's love in me), I gain nothing.
>
> Love endures long and is patient and kind; love never is envious
> nor boils over with jealousy, is not boastful or vainglorious,
> does not display itself haughtily.
>
> It is not conceited (arrogant and inflated with pride); it is not
> rude (unmannerly) and does not act unbecomingly. Love (God's
> love in us) does not insist on its own rights or its own way, for
> it is not self-seeking; it is not touchy or fretful or resentful; it
> takes no account of the evil done to it [it pays no attention to a
> suffered wrong]. (1 Corinthians 13:1-5 AMP)

I hope you have internalized these Bible verses, for they alone can bring sanity to a society full of broken relationships. Let's not just talk about love; let's practice real love. Love is light in a world full of darkness. No wonder the Bible says that love, an intense and unfailing love, covers a multitude of sins. (See 1 Peter 4:8.) Whoever is incapable of divine love, is spiritually impotent, or dead.

As a faith family, God wants us to live sacrificially for our fellow believers, and not just for ourselves (1 John 3:16). By Christ's death, we have come to progressively recognize and understand, the nature of selfless love by which Jesus sacrificed His life for us. This is an example of experiential love, worthy of our emulation.

The unspiritual mind, however, does not accept these principles, but rejects them as weaknesses and contrary to human intuition. I came across an article on the Internet, *"Is Your Marriage Ripe for an Affair?"* which dealt with why spouses stray. I found it fascinating to learn that couples are encouraged to have a built-in exit strategy in their relationships. According to the article, true intimacy requires two people having independent lives, and so having one person live selflessly for the other person is counter-intuitive given today's harsh reality of marriage partnerships.

Some see love as an unrealistic expectation. To "affair-proof a marriage," the article suggests, since there are no guarantees in marriage, getting a life is very important.

> When you have your own sense of income and independence, and feel that you can be with or without him, he will smell it and he'll treat you differently…. Create a rich, rewarding life for yourself and if your spouse did have an affair and ultimately leave you, you would be well equipped to cope. The only person you can count on to always be there is you. Being abandoned by a spouse is far preferable to abandoning yourself.

> All the propaganda in the world tells us 'keep your man,' 'hold on to your man,' 'jump through hoops for your man,' but your attitude should be 'If you want to go, I'll help you pack'.
> *(Is Your Marriage Ripe for an Affair* http://women.msn.com)

The unspiritual mind is an unregenerate mind and so cannot accept the things of God. In Paul's letters to the Corinthians, and Romans he explained:

> But the natural, nonspiritual man does not accept or welcome or admit into his heart the gifts and teachings and revelations of the Spirit of God, for they are folly (meaningless nonsense) to him; and he is incapable of knowing them [of progressively recognizing, understanding, and becoming better acquainted with them] because they are spiritually discerned and estimated and appreciated.          (1 Corinthians 2:14 AMP)

> For those who are according to the flesh and are controlled by its unholy desires set their minds on and pursue those things which gratify the flesh, but those who are according to the Spirit and are controlled by the desires of the Spirit set their minds on and seek those things which gratify the [Holy] Spirit.

> Now the mind of the flesh [which is sense and reason without the Holy Spirit] is death [death that comprises all the miseries arising from sin, both here and hereafter]. But the mind of the [Holy] Spirit is life and [soul] peace [both now and forever].

> [That is] because the mind of the flesh [with its carnal thoughts and purposes] is hostile to God, for it does not submit itself to God's Law; indeed it cannot.          Romans 8:5-7 AMP)

> For the god of this world has blinded the unbelievers' minds [that they should not discern the truth], preventing them from seeing the illuminating light of the Gospel of the glory of Christ (the Messiah), Who is the Image and Likeness of God.
> (2 Corinthians 4:4 AMP)

Today we live in a society where narcissism (self-love), or our desire to be somebody, is responsible for most marital anomalies, to undermining the marriage institution and family relationships. What are the characteristics of narcissism? Clinical psychologists define Pathological Narcissism Disorder (PND) as:

> A pattern of traits and behaviours, which signify infatuation and obsession with one's self to the exclusion of all others and the egotistic and ruthless pursuit of one's gratification, dominance and ambition.
> (www.healthyplace.com/communities/personality_Disorders)

According to Dr. Vaknin, most narcissists (75 percent) are men. Below are some of the signs to spot a narcissist before it is too late:

1. Displays haughty behavior

2. Has a tendency to humiliate, criticize, and belittle others

3. Has a tendency to exaggerate, *and tell* small, unnecessary lies

4. Has a tendency to fantasize about unlimited success

5. Brags incessantly, ignores you, does not listen

6. Has a tendency to idealize you beyond the call of courtship

7. Makes promises that are incommensurate either with the event, or with his ability to fulfill them

8. Has haughty body language

(http://www.healthyplace.com/Communities/Personality_Disorders/ narcissism/faq58.html)

## Self-aggrandizement

Self-aggrandizement is the desire to be somebody. The antithesis of our desire to be somebody is low self-esteem. Nobody wants to be put down because our egos demand that we be put on a pedestal. Our self-aggrandizement tendencies are not bad per se, but can easily be misplaced, resulting in the sin of pride. Satan is the father of pride; in fact, it was pride that got him into trouble with God. Satan, who is the god of this world, has blinded a lot of people into thinking that they don't need God. In essence, he makes people believe that they are their own gods. The spiritual philosophy of the universal consciousness, as preached by New Agers, denies the existence of a named God. They believe in a divine force that lives in each of us and connects everybody. To them, discovering who you really are, and not having someone broker between you and this unnamed, divine power, is key to attaining enlightenment and to becoming one with this universal consciousness, whatever you choose to call it.

This distorts the truth of our spirituality and our accountability to a personified Maker. This is a clever way to tell people that they are masters of their own destinies. On the surface it sounds palatable, but pushed to its logical conclusion, what they are saying is that there is no God or the devil, but only negative and positive forces, with a mind or consciousness. This line of thinking has given impetus to the "Me, Myself, and I" religion that says through reason and hard work, you can achieve your dreams without any divine providence of a heavenly Father. This mentality has led to numerous self-help books, to fuel the self-aggrandizement and pride of an individual. But according to Proverbs 16:25, "There is a way that seems right to a man, but in the end it leads to death." To those who believe there is no God, listen to what the Psalmist says:

> The [empty-headed] fool has said in his heart, There is no God. Corrupt and evil are they, and doing abominable iniquity; there is none who does good.
>
> God looked down from heaven upon the children of men to see if there were any who understood, who sought (inquired after and desperately required) God.
>
> Every one of them has gone back [backslidden and fallen away]; they have altogether become filthy and corrupt; there is none who does good, no, not one.        (Psalm 53:1-3 AMP)

## The Sin of Pride Begins With "I Will"

According to the Bible, Satan fell as a result of pride. The sins of Satan and the sins of mankind originate with the same concept: "I will" instead of "thy will (meaning God's will) be done." An account is given of the fall of Satan as written in Isaiah:

> How art thou fallen from heaven, O Lucifer, son of the morning!
>
> How art thou cut down to the ground, which didst weaken the nations! For thou hast said in thine heart,
>
> I will ascend into heaven,

I will exalt my throne above the stars of God:

I will sit also upon the mount of the congregation, in the sides of the north:

I will ascend above the heights of the clouds;

I will be like the most High.

Yet thou shalt be brought down to hell, to the sides of the pit. They that see thee shall narrowly look upon thee, and consider thee, saying,

Is this the man that made the earth to tremble, that did shake kingdoms; That made the world as a wilderness, and destroyed the cities thereof; that opened not the house of his prisoners?

(Isaiah 14:12-17)

Satan, the enemy of all mankind, encourages the expression of the dark or negative sides of our humanity. Where he does not succeed, he joins the good side and torpedoes it to the extreme with legality, pride, or self-righteousness. The self-righteous man does not see his imperfections and faults, but blames other people for their faults.

Similarly, our good deeds are often stained with self-interest and our demand for justice are nothing but our lust for retribution. When we are offended, revenge and our insistence on obtaining our "pound of flesh" become the norm.

Sometimes, people do things in the name of organized religion or faith, but on close scrutiny, they are in violation of the spirit and intent of that faith or religion. True servants of our Lord Jesus Christ should shy away from opulence and concentrate on propagating the Gospel. Disregarding this advice sends the wrong message about the church and its mission. No wonder today, people see charismatic churches as a moneymaking machine rather than an evangelical institution. A servant of God should act as servants do--serve.

As a servant of God, be careful of the lust of the eyes, the lust of the flesh, and the pride of life, or you may be compelled to choose between God and mammon (see Matthew 6:24-25). If you chose to serve mammon don't blame God for your financial blessings. Be careful, and don't become like Adam who told God, "The woman whom thou gavest to be with me, she gave me of the tree, and I did eat" (Genesis 3:12). Your money should be used to glorify God, and not to satisfy Self. It is your responsibility to steer clear away from temptations. Be careful of your role as a servant, and don't act like a rich ruler or prince by lording it over the saints.

Nowadays, the enemy has stepped in to inflame the spiritual pride, self-aggrandizement, and egoistic tendencies of our church leaders in a capitalistic society, where material prosperity has become the yardstick of human success. But in the end, this is what Jesus will tell them:

> Not everyone who says to me, "Lord, Lord," will enter the kingdom of heaven, but only he who does the will of my Father who is in heaven. Many will say to me on that day, "Lord, Lord," did we not prophesy in your name, and in your name drive out demons and perform many miracles?' Then I will tell them plainly, "I never knew you. Away from me, you evildoers!"
>
> (Matthew 7:21-23 NIV)

I have likened the dysfunctional or egotistical relationship of "self" to an autoimmune disease, a cancerous phenomenon familiar to medical professionals. The word *auto* is the Greek word for "self." The immune system is a network of complicated cells and cell components that normally work to defend the body and eliminate infectious diseases caused by bacteria, viruses, or other invading microbes. If a person has an autoimmune disease, the immune system mistakenly attacks the body, targeting the cells, tissues, and organs of a person's body, resulting in an inflammation of the affected site. Pride and self-love are nothing but inflated egos. They hurt, do no good to self or society, and only serve to infuriate God.

Pride in any form is spiritually and physically deadly. Ask King Herod, and he will tell you that being eaten alive by worms is a high price to pay for trying to usurp God's glory. (Acts 12:22-23.)

# How Do We Rise Above Pride?

In a relationship, whereas men tend to see love as playful or a game, women see love as emotional, storgic and pragmatic. Men therefore see their wives as naggers, and the wives are upset at husbands for playing games with their emotional needs.

Often in most marriages, an attack on our self-esteem or self-aggrandizement can lead to spousal abuse. Misplaced self-identity can also be a cause for insecurity to adversely affect the partnership. People tend to lash out when they feel threatened or insecure. In situations like these, although counseling may help, if the source of the attack is spiritual, only spiritual counseling and prayers are the appropriate therapeutic interventions, not human wisdom. The true antidote to pride and arrogance is contrition and humility. God is pleased with humility and a contrite heart. They are magnets that attract His divine blessings. Virtues such as these make marriage and family relationships stronger, prosperous, and longer lasting. The Bible therefore warns:

> Do nothing out of selfish ambition or vain conceit, but in humility consider others better than yourselves.
> (Philippians 2:3)

> Before his downfall a man's heart is proud, but humility comes before honor. Humility and the fear of the LORD bring wealth and honor and life. (Proverbs 18:12; Proverbs 22:4)

You have often heard the slogan, "God helps those who help themselves." This is non-biblical. God helps those who help other people. Carefully note this spiritual principle: It is when you take care of other people that your needs are met. According to the Scriptures, *"A generous man will prosper; he who refreshes others will himself be refreshed" (Proverbs 11:25).* The prayer of young King Solomon for wisdom to lead God's people, and Hannah's prayers to offer her son in the service of God, brought instant results. In our personal relationships, we rise above pride when we look to the needs of others. We rise above pride when we keep our promises. When we are wrong, we say we are sorry and don't blame others for things that go wrong. We rise above pride when we are able to defer to others, not wanting to always be in charge or win, to have our way, or have the last word. May God help us all!

When people are faced with temptation, three things normally affect the decision they make. First, there is the inner divine conscience telling them not to do it. Second, a contrary voice says, "Go ahead. It's no big deal. Everybody does it." Or, "Are you going to stand by and take this disrespect and abuse?" The contrary voice will always urge you to take care of yourself first, before anyone else, in tune with worldly wisdom and philosophies. Finally, there is free will (one of the components of our divine nature), our freedom to choose to do either what is right, or wrong. But remember, there is God's will, and there is devil's will. Don't align your will to the devil's:

> Be very careful, then, how you live--not as unwise but as wise, making the most of every opportunity, because the days are evil. Therefore do not be foolish, but understand what the Lord's will is.                              (Ephesians 5:15-17 NIV)

The devil operates by deceit and slander. Look at how he attacked and slandered Job. In the book of Job we read:

> Now there was a day when the sons of God came to present themselves before the LORD, and Satan came also among them.

> And the LORD said unto Satan, Whence comest thou? Then Satan answered the LORD, and said, From going to and fro in the earth, and from walking up and down in it.

> And the LORD said unto Satan, Hast thou considered my servant Job, that there is none like him in the earth, a perfect and an upright man, one that feareth God, and escheweth evil?

> Then Satan answered the LORD, and said, Doth Job fear God for nought?

> Hast not thou made an hedge about him, and about his house,

> and about all that he hath on every side? Thou hast blessed the work of his hands, and his substance is increased in the land.
>
> But put forth thine hand now, and touch all that he hath, and he will curse thee to thy face.
>
> And the LORD said unto Satan, Behold, all that he hath is in thy power; only upon himself put not forth thine hand. So Satan went forth from the presence of the LORD.        (Job 1:6-12)

At times God wants to show us off to the world. But can our testimony stand scrutiny? Humans are made in the image of God; therefore, God respects the choices we make. But He expects us to make right choices based on what He has endowed in our humanity.

In Proverbs 27:17, we are told that as iron sharpens iron, so one man sharpens another. Moreover, bad company corrupts good character (1 Corinthians 15:33), so we are advised not to be unequally yoked to unbelievers (2 Corinthians 6:14). Be careful of evil friends in disguise to lead you astray, with worldly philosophies that question the wisdom of God as found in the Bible.

The devil and his agents are working feverishly to entice you to do things that are contrary to the will of God. Anything he touches breeds death, and no human institution, including the church, is immune. His destructive handiwork is seen all over the world. He knows his time is short as we draw closer to the end of this age, when he will be confined to the eternal lake of fire in hell. He has therefore intensified his onslaught on the family structure in general, and the marriage institution in particular. How does the devil hopes to accomplish his grand designs?

Let's go to the beginning, to the Garden of Eden, to the tree of the knowledge of good and evil, when human beings became imprinted with the knowledge of good and evil after they ate the forbidden fruit. Man's desire for self-aggrandizement, to put man first before God, triggered the sin of disobedience. God granted that wish, so it is with us today. The freedom of choice to chose between God and the Devil, between good or evil. But there will be no room for the old self in God's kingdom as it was the case before man was driven out of paradise. Satan therefore seeks to latch on to our evil components, to buffet, sift, and devour us especially, by elevating the status of "self" in our relationship, as written:

> For people will be lovers of self and [utterly] self-centered, lovers of money and aroused by an inordinate [greedy] desire for wealth, proud and arrogant and contemptuous boasters. They will be abusive (blasphemous, scoffing), disobedient to parents, ungrateful, unholy and profane. [They will be] without natural [human] affection (callous and inhuman), relentless (admitting of no truce or appeasement); [they will be] slanderers (false accusers, troublemakers), intemperate and loose in morals and conduct, uncontrolled and fierce, haters of good. [They will be] treacherous [betrayers], rash, [and] inflated with self-conceit. [They will be] lovers of sensual pleasures and vain amusements more than and rather than lovers of God. (2 Timothy 3:2-4 AMP)

This is precisely what is taking place in our society today, and it is going to get worse. It is only by the grace and mercy of God that our relationships have not disintegrated to that of the animal kingdom. Good always triumphs over evil because God is still in control. We are reminded that: "Where sin increased and abounded, grace (God's unmerited favor) has surpassed it and increased the more and super abounded" according to (Romans 5:20 AMP).

In a nutshell, be careful of the times. Be mindful of the on-going spiritual war between the seed of the woman and that of the serpent. Demonic forces can overpower a person, brainwash, and blind him or her to the truth. Therefore, be vigilant of the power struggles in your relationships. In your marriage and family relationships, do you compromise with each other, or do you compete and control?

Next, we will consider the origins of illicit spiritual unions and how demonic third parties have infiltrated and interfered with our relationships. In the subsequent chapters, we will examine some of the reasons why people are caught in cycles of domestic violence and turmoil, and its effect on the quality of life within today's marriages and family settings.

# Chapter Three

## Origins of Illicit Spiritual Unions

The Bible gives us an account of the origin of demonic spiritual marriages.

> And it came to pass, when men began to multiply on the face of the earth, and daughters were born unto them; That the sons of God saw the daughters of men that they were fair; and they took them wives of all which they chose. There were giants in the earth in those days; and also after that, when the sons of God came in unto the daughters of men, and they bare children to them, the same became mighty men which were of old, men of renown.                (Genesis 6:1, 2, 4 NIV)

The sons of God were the fallen angels who, along with Satan, were cast out of heaven. These angels engaged in illicit sexual unions with the daughters of men and went after strange flesh, and God was very displeased about the contamination. In fact God was so angry He severely punished the angels who had committed these sexual atrocities by banishing them to the abyss.

> And the angels which kept not their first estate, but left their own habitation, he hath reserved in everlasting chains under darkness unto the judgment of the great day.
>
> Even as Sodom and Gomorrah, and the cities about them in like manner, giving themselves over to fornication, and going

> after strange flesh, are set forth for an example, suffering the
> vengeance of eternal fire. (Jude 1:6-7)

God created human beings out of dust and water, and He breathed into man and he became a living soul (Genesis 2:7). Man was created after the image of God. Angels however, were created out of wind and fire as ministering beings. In Hebrews we read, "Referring to the angels He says, [God] Who makes His angels winds and His ministering servants flames of fire" (Hebrews 1:7 AMP).

The crossbreed that resulted from the sexual union of humans and angelic beings were the Nephilim (Anakites) in the days of Noah. These Nephilim were giants, very barbaric and evil. Together with man had become corrupted with wickedness, so God decided to wipe all mankind off the face of the earth with the exception of Noah and his family of eight (i.e.; Noah and his wife, their three sons, and their wives) were spared from the flood that destroyed the earth.

The union of the angelic beings, and humans resulted in a different kind of spirit, a "contaminated spirit." These evil spirits started to cause trouble for humans. They started to afflict, oppress, attack, do battle, and to destroy the earth. The contamination and the resultant spiritual marriages may have produced so much confusion, chaos, and wickedness that it grieved God. His heart was filled with pain. From the Bible, we read that every inclination of man's heart was evil all the time and so God decided to destroy the world. God, in Genesis 6:3, said, *"My Spirit shall not always thrive with man, for that he also is flesh."* Today this sentiment is echoed in the warning Paul gave the Galatians. He told them:

> But I say, walk and live [habitually] in the [Holy] Spirit [responsive to and controlled and guided by the Spirit]; then you will certainly not gratify the cravings and desires of the flesh (of human nature without God). For the desires of the flesh are opposed to the [Holy] Spirit, and the [desires of the] Spirit are opposed to the flesh (godless human nature); for these are antagonistic to each other [continually withstanding and in conflict with each other], so that you are not free but are prevented from doing what you desire to do.
> (Galatians 5:16-17 AMP)

40

# Sexuality and the Desires of Demons

In the Garden of Eden, the serpent seduced the woman to eat the forbidden fruit. God therefore cursed the serpent and said:

> I'm declaring war between you and the Woman, between your offspring and hers. He'll wound your head, you'll wound his heel.                    (Genesis 3:15 MSG)

The curse that was put on Satan and his offspring is still in effect. These evil spirits are bruising the heels of mankind. They have risen up against the children of men, the offspring of the woman, particularly against women because the curse was issued directly to the serpent and the woman. You often hear the term the "brides of Satan" with regard to occultism. (Brown, Rebecca MD, He Came To Set The Captives Free, 1986, pg. 61.) It is a spiritual phenomenon and a physical reality. It is an illicit spiritual marriage, involving acts of sexual intercourse with evil spiritual entities.

Sex was meant for the enjoyment among humans. However, the magnetism of sex is so strong that even the fallen angels could not resist going after beautiful women. Besides, it is one of the easiest ways to become one with humans and their seeds or descendants. Through sex, evil spirits gain a foothold and establish strongholds in an individual, family or clan to spiritually overpower them. Pray to loose yourself of all ancestral spiritual negativities.

R. J. Adams, a Bible commentator, has suggested that the bodies of the giants or Nephilims were destroyed in the flood, but God permitted their spirits to remain on earth as demons and evil spirits, harassing, tormenting, and destroying human lives until their appointed time to be confined in the eternal lake of fire. It is my speculation that while Satan and the fallen angels constitute the top hierarchy of the kingdom of darkness (principalities, powers, and rulers), the demonic spirits of human origin serve as the foot soldiers to carry out direct and personal assaults against mankind, especially, women. These demonic spirits, still have human desires, and lust that

41

cannot be fulfilled unless they enter into human bodies. Where they cannot inhabit people, they follow them around to harass and cause confusion. God therefore warns us to flee all sexual improprieties, and uncleanness. I am sure by now you are beginning to understand why certain marriages, and relationships are doomed from the start, or don't work out.

Man was created in the image of God. Man, therefore holds a unique position in God's creation. We are told that the saints will one day judge the world and angels:

> Do you not know that the saints (the believers) will [one day] judge and govern the world? And if the world [itself] is to be judged and ruled by you, are you unworthy and incompetent to try [such petty matters] of the smallest courts of justice?
>
> Do you not know also that we [Christians] are to judge the [very] angels and pronounce opinion between right and wrong [for them]? How much more then [as to] matters pertaining to this world and of this life only!     (1 Corinthians 6:2-3 AMP)

Here on earth Jesus has also given us the authority and power over evil spirits and to cure diseases according to the Gospel of Luke 9:1.

## Demons Work in Clusters

Demons work in clusters. There are many cluster groups of demons, but I will concentrate on two of the most destructive groups, bent on disrupting and destroying the marriage institution and other family relationships in the world. Let us look at the two strongmen of these cluster groups: the spirit of jealousy, and the spirit of heaviness or depression. These two tend to operate from opposing ends of the spectrum. There are exceptional cases, as in murder-suicide, where both ends of the spectrum seem to strongly reside in the individual.

On Saturday March 12, 2005 Terry Ratzman a forty four-year-old computer technician, opened fire, killing seven people, including his pastor, before turning the gun on himself. He was a member of the Brookfield, Wisconsin, Living Church of God, a splinter group of the

Worldwide Church of God. Mr. Ratzman was apparently grappling with an impending job loss. He was also known to have reacted negatively to something that was said at a February 26 sermon, which caused him to storm out in anger. Some who knew him said he had bouts with depression. One church member is quoted as saying, "He was always kind of weird and standoffish. He never did anything physically violent, but he could say things very sharply."(www.columbiatribune.com/2005/Mar/20050314News021.asp)

Rapid, or clinical mood swings are nothing but demons playing ball. Psychological problems are nothing but the manifestations of spiritual suppression and oppression of the mind, the emotions, and ultimately of behavior. Be careful: anger and depression don't mix! No one is immune, not even Bible-believing churchgoers. Those who mistake or misdiagnose demonic attacks for treatable clinical depression are bound to encounter situations similar to what happened to Mr. Raztman. If the spiritual is more powerful than the physical, why not seek the spiritual first before the physical?

## Spirit of Jealousy

Jealousy is a spirit. In Numbers, we read about the spirit of jealousy possessing, or influencing a man. God told Moses:

> Speak to the sons of Israel and say to them, 'If any man's wife goes astray and is unfaithful to him, and a man has intercourse with her and it is hidden from the eyes of her husband and she is undetected, although she has defiled herself, and there is no witness against her and she has not been caught in the act, if a spirit of jealousy comes over him and he is jealous of his wife when she has defiled herself, or if a spirit of jealousy comes over him and he is jealous of his wife when she has not defiled herself...                    (Numbers 5:11-14 NASB)

We all have gates or doorways to our spirits. In Revelation 3:20, Jesus stands at our door, knocking to see if we would invite Him to come in and have fellowship with us. But Jesus is not the only one knocking. Sin, and evil spirits are also crouching and waiting for an opportunity to conquer our doors or gates. It is imperative that we only invite Jesus. If we don't, the strongman who usually controls the gate to our soul when a stronghold has been established will allow other spirits either to enter or prevent others from entering. In Proverbs 27:4, we read, "Anger is cruel, and wrath is like a flood, but who can survive the destructiveness of jealousy?" Jesus said we would know the strongmen by their fruits. The fruits (or symptoms) of jealousy include but are not limited to the following:

| | | |
|---|---|---|
| Lust of the eyes | Intolerance | Name-Calling |
| Lust of the flesh | Rejection | Infantilizing |
| Prince Charming | Lying | Humiliating |
| Envy | Promise and Fail | Restricting |
| Possessiveness | Accusation of others | Anger |
| Contention | Blaming | Rage |
| Strife | Suspicion | Screaming |
| Extreme Competition | Questioning | Insulting |
| Resentment | Chronic Degrading | Revenge |
| Divisions | Coercion and Threats | Spite |
| Isolation, | Ridiculing | Cruelty |
| Domineering spirit | Unforgiveness | Hatred |
| Control | Slander | Murder |

## Spirit of Heaviness

The spirit of heaviness is the counterpart of jealousy, the receiver in a "donor receiver" relationship. One is the oppressor, and the other, the suppressed. However, both are victims of the same demonic source, playing one partner against the other in a "lose lose" situation to cause commotion, to torment, and to break up marriages and families.

The fruits of the spirit of heaviness, and depression include:

| | | |
|---|---|---|
| Despair | Dejection | Torn Spirit |
| Sorrow | Hopelessness | Excessive-mourning |
| Grief | Guilt | Insomnia |
| Self-pity | Neglect | Suicidal thoughts |
| Rejection | Depression | Self-destruction |
| Broken-heartedness | Inner Hurts | Confusion |
| Frustration | Heaviness | Suicide |

The dynamics of these assaults on the marital union is manifested as squabbles where one of the partners is always angry and nasty, bossy and supersensitive, enraged and fearful, bitter and depressed, or isolated and despondent. The most lethal of these combinations is the person who is always depressed and angry. But God is our refuge and help, to grant consolation and joy.

> And provide for those who grieve in Zion-- to bestow on them a crown of beauty instead of ashes, the oil of gladness instead of mourning, and a garment of praise instead of a spirit of despair. They will be called oaks of righteousness, a planting of the LORD for the display of his splendor.        (Isaiah 61:3 NIV)

I like this verse because it tells us the antidote to depression or heaviness of heart. Ashes denote brokenness, disappointments, pain, bitterness, and what is left of our dreams. In short, we don't hold onto our ashes, or wallow in self-pity. Depression tends to sap our vitality, and leaves us dry. One of the insidious tactics of the devil is to gradually wear out the saints with worry, anxiety, and the cares of this world, to disappoint and depress them. The Bible tells us that a cheerful heart is good medicine for our souls, but a crushed spirit dries up the bones (Proverbs 17:22). In the Bible when God inflicted King Saul with a spirit of depression, David played his harp and the evil spirit departed.

> And it came to pass, when the evil spirit from God was upon Saul, that David took an harp, and played with his hand: so Saul was refreshed, and was well, and the evil spirit departed from him.                        (1 Samuel 16:23)

Surround yourself with praise and thanksgiving to God. For those who grieve and are depressed, be reminded, "the joy of the LORD is your strength" (Nehemiah 8:10). When you take your eyes off Jesus and focus on your problems, or even on your wealth, true happiness and joy become an elusive mirage.

Money is a defense, and so is wisdom, but only true wisdom (Jesus Christ) gives the superabundant life, here on earth and eternity (Ecclesiastes 7:12). Those who have left matrimonial homes on the pretext of finding true happiness and joy in other relationships deceive themselves. It is only through the joy of the Lord in your life that you will truly strengthen and enrich your marriage.

The devil likes to play games with our minds and hearts by feeding us with partial truths that lead to nothing but jilted love, frustration grieve, despair, and depression. Be vigilant! Let the Holy Spirit be your Comforter.

In a family, the same demons that cause the breakup of the marriage also follow the children. Those with no partnership skills or proper communications skills to negotiate, resolve, or make decisions together in order to soften the spiritual onslaught on the marriage, find themselves caught in a vicious cycle where one partner always complains and attacks, while the other retreats and ignores. This too is the work of the enemy.

In spiritual warfare the whole household comes under attack. The key lies in how one handles stress when under spiritual attack. How prepared are you to handle the stress of marriage and to spiritually defend your family when under attack? A review of your family history may reveal a generational curse or spiritual attacks, where for example marriages in the family tend to end in divorce.

The dynamic of these spiritual attacks are also such that if dad treated Mom with disrespect, Junior learns to do the same thing. He will either become rebellious and undermine Mom's authority structure or grow up to resent Dad for the way he treated Mom. The irony is that, although Junior may have resented the way dad treated Mom, he cannot resist mistreating his wife the way Dad did. Why this anomaly? Be wary of spiritual enforcers assigned to make sure that there is no peace in your family. They will follow, monitor, and police you everywhere you go to enforce, any curses operating in your life.

Oprah did a show called "Inside Prison: Why Women Murder." A segment of the show was based on Liz Garbus's documentary, *Girlhood.* Two girls, an eighteen-year-old and a nineteen-year-old, spent years in a juvenile home. For three years, cameras followed them, and their story was turned into a film. For our entire lives, we all have spiritual lenses strain on us, both good, and evil.

> Then I saw a great white throne and him who was seated on it. Earth and sky fled from his presence, and there was no place for them. And I saw the dead, great and small, standing before the throne, and books were opened. Another book was opened, which is the book of life. The dead were judged according to what they had done as recorded in the books. The sea gave up the dead that were in it, and death and Hades gave up the dead that were in them, and each person was judged according to what he had done. (Revelation 20:11-13 NIV)

During the interview, Oprah asked the nineteen-year-old, if she had anybody, and she said, "spirit." Oprah then asked, "You mean God?" She said, "No." Oprah obviously wanted to help the girl, but she walked off the set before the show was over. Without any spiritual intervention, it will be hard for this girl to maintain any meaningful relationships.

I don't know the particular situation of this nineteen-year-old, but in many cases, actual demons or spirits are directly in touch with their victims. These spirits will not allow their captives to accept any help to put them back on their feet. Instead, they drive them into isolation, where nobody can help them. These people become unsociable recluse. Spiritually, their spirits may be in the tombs or graveyard. Day and night they scream to be set free. But just like the demon-possessed man of Gadara (see Mark chapter 5), an encounter with Jesus changes everything. The light of His glory will shine on them, and they will run to His feet and worship Him. When you worship Jesus, He sets you loose. Whoever the Son sets free shall be free indeed (John 8:36).

## Ancestral Covenants and our Stolen Blessings

Some of our ancestors sold their souls to the devil in exchange for prosperity, and protection for themselves, and their descendants. However, the spirits that were called upon to protect family members at times took advantage of the women. They interfered with their abilities to find a soul mate, or to bear and raise children. If you are struggling to fulfill any of these destiny-oriented tasks, you need spiritual solutions to your problems.

Sometimes these spirits send agents or "contrary spirits" into the lives of these women. When that happens, they find themselves attracted to wrong mates, often resulting in heart-breaking, disastrous marriages and, in the process, destroying the family. God is the one who created the marriage institution; therefore, any anti-marriage forces walls of marital partition must be brought down and removed. If you are having problems attracting a suitable mate, and you feel you are experiencing lateness in marriage, stand on the Word of God. Declare, decree, and command that what God has said must come to pass in your situation. Stand on the following verse in Isaiah:

> Seek out of the book of the Lord and read: not one of these [details of prophecy] shall fail, none shall want and lack her mate [in fulfillment]. For the mouth [of the Lord] has commanded, and His Spirit has gathered them.        Isaiah 34:16 AMP)

> Therefore say unto them, Thus saith the Lord GOD; There shall none of my words be prolonged any more, but the word which I have spoken shall be done, saith the Lord GOD.
> (Ezekiel 12:28)

It is through the family that God blesses people. Listen to what God said to Abraham:

> And I will establish my covenant between me and thee and thy seed after thee in their generations for an everlasting covenant, to be a God unto thee, and to thy seed after thee. And God said, Sarah thy wife shall bear thee a son indeed; and thou shalt call his name Isaac: and I will establish my covenant with him for an everlasting covenant, and with his seed after him.
> (Genesis 17:7, 19)

> That in blessing I will bless thee, and in multiplying I will multiply thy seed as the stars of the heaven, and as the sand which is upon the sea shore; and thy seed shall possess the gate of his enemies.        (Genesis 22:17)

Through the seed of His people, God will also raise an army to fight Satan, and his demonic forces here on earth. Therefore, the spiritual covering over a family is important, and that covering is usually stronger when both parents are together. It is a parent's duty and responsibility to stand in the gap, and provide spiritual covering for their children. Always pray and commit your children to God's care.

For men, finances matter a great deal. We want to be able to take care of our families. The devil therefore likes to touch our finances and undermine our abilities to be the breadwinner. People make so much money, but at the end of the year they don't understand where all their money goes. These men are broke or always in debt. They are often passed over for promotions. Better jobs are hard to come by, and growth in all areas of their lives is stagnated. They seem to take one step forward and two steps back. If you're a born-again believer and you are not living in sin, the harassment may be demonic. But have faith. God is God, and no matter what your situation, He can turn it around and use it to His glory.

Another favorite area of demonic attack is our health. Some families are plagued with mind problems, cancer, alcoholism, premature death, or chronic diseases. Some only understand the explanation for these situations in terms of genetics, fate, and sheer bad luck. Sickness and diseases can be inherited as a result of an evil inheritance, a form of generational curse.

## Evil Family Inheritance

During a deliverance ministration in the Bronx, a pastor revealed to one lady that, years ago one of her ancestors, a hunter by trade, went to the forest to hunt. He shot down an animal; however, when he approached the animal, it got up and blew air into the face of the hunter and put him under its spell. The animal opened its mouth, and the hunter put his hand in. When he drew it out, it was full of saliva. Spiritually, the saliva was used to inflict fibroids among the women in the family. He put his hand into the animal's mouth again, and when he drew it out, it was full of rings, which symbolized the marriages in the family. For this family, the women would be afflicted with fibroids and their marriages put under a curse. The women, no matter how beautiful, would not be able to marry or sustain any meaningful marriage barring spiritual or divine intervention. This may sound preposterous, but what does the devil wants from us? To steal, kill, and destroy.

The Bible says that the sins of the fathers will be visited on their children to the fourth generation and sometimes to the tenth generation. (See Deuteronomy 5:9-10; Exodus 20:4-6). A classic example of an evil inheritance in the Bible is the case of Gehazi, the servant of Elisha. When Gehazi disobeyed Elisha and took gifts from Naaman, Elisha cursed Gehazi, saying:

> The leprosy therefore of Naaman shall cleave unto thee, and unto thy seed forever. And he went out from his presence a leper as white as snow. (2 Kings 5:27)

If you are suffering from genetic sickness, your problem could be spiritual. A review of your family history could reveal that long ago your ancestors were involved in some form of pagan worship or violated some covenants, and these have unleashed curses on your family, giving demonic spirits free reign of terror from one generation to another. The apostle Paul, in Ephesians 6:12 reminds us of our fight against spiritual wickedness in high places. When you ignore his warning, or take lightly what Jesus said concerning the devil, evil spirits have a field day, devastating and decimating your family with all kinds of afflictions and calamities. The curse must be broken before anyone can be set free from this family pattern of evil inheritance.

We serve a living God, an omnipotent God, whose Word is Spirit and life. There is power, healing, and deliverance in the Word of God. Let us therefore, in one accord, pray with the psalmist, a prayer of agreement and say:

> Bless the LORD, O my soul: and all that is within me, bless his holy name. Bless the LORD, O my soul, and forget not all his benefits: Who forgiveth all thine iniquities; who healeth all thy diseases; Who redeemeth thy life from destruction; who crowneth thee with lovingkindness and tender mercies.
>
> (Psalm 103:1-4)

Have faith: God's Word is already settled in heaven! Therefore He watches to perform it. If you are having marital problems, the likelihood of interference from a demonic third-party spirit to your marriage, is very high. These spirits are unrelenting and diabolical, and would do anything just to break up the marriage, or keep you from marrying. Satan and his demonic hordes enjoy breaking up marriages, especially Christian marriages. But the Bible says, what God has joined together let no one put asunder (Matthew 19:6). Stand on God's promise and claim your deliverance.

But be warned, you cannot be set free if you yield your body and faculties as instruments of sin to do as you please. Your body has a spiritual purpose. Find out what it is and obey.

# Chapter Four

## Honor God with Your Body

*Know ye not that the unrighteous shall not inherit the kingdom of God? Be not deceived: neither fornicators, nor idolaters [those who give supreme attention to anything other than God], nor adulterers, nor effeminate, nor abusers of themselves with mankind.*

*Flee fornication. Every sin that a man doeth is without the body; but he that committeth fornication sinneth against his own body. What? know ye not that your body is the temple of the Holy Ghost which is in you, which ye have of God, and ye are not your own? For ye are bought with a price: therefore glorify God in your body, and in your spirit, which are God's. (1 Corinthians 6:9, 18-20, comments added)*

In chapter 2, we discussed the fact that human beings are part spiritual and part human. However, since our Maker is spiritual, wouldn't it appeal to the logical mind to seek after the spiritual? The way I see it, anything we do without any spiritual significance to glorify our Maker, who is spiritual, is worthless. Jesus told His disciples:

> It is the Spirit Who gives life [He is the Life-giver]; the flesh conveys no benefit whatever [there is no profit in it]. The words

> (truths) that I have been speaking to you are spirit and life. But
> [still] some of you fail to believe and trust and have faith. For
> Jesus knew from the first who did not believe and had no faith
> and who would betray Him and be false to Him.
>
> (John 6:63-64 AMP)

Our sexuality and our spirituality are part of what make us who we are as humans. Anybody violating his or her sexuality is putting himself or herself in deep trouble spiritually.

The Bible exhorts us to avoid all forms of sexual immorality and impurities, because they are some of the ways by which we defile our bodies--the temple of God for Christians. Often the divine nature of man, is in conflict with his dust or animal nature, so we are advised to live wisely:

> So I say, live by the Spirit, and you will not gratify the desires of
> the sinful nature. For the sinful nature desires what is contrary
> to the Spirit, and the Spirit what is contrary to the sinful nature.
> They are in conflict with each other, so that you do not do what
> you want. But if the Spirit leads you, you are not under law
> *(which condemns us)*.
>
> The acts of the sinful nature are obvious: sexual immorality,
> impurity and debauchery; idolatry and witchcraft; hatred,
> discord, jealousy, fits of rage, selfish ambition, dissensions,
> factions and envy; drunkenness, orgies *(swinging)*, and the
> like. I warn you, as I did before, that those who live like this
> will not inherit the kingdom of God.
>
> (Galatians 5:16-21, *comments added*)

The spiritual mystery in sex is that, when you have sex with someone, a spiritual exchange takes place between both parties as written: "What? Know ye not that he, which is joined to an harlot, is one body? For two, saith he, shall be one flesh. But he that is joined unto the Lord is one spirit." (1 Corinthians 6.16:17)

When you engage in sex outside marriage, or in sexual immoralities you become unholy. According to the Bible, without holiness no one can see God. Sexual sins can therefore prevent you from inheriting God's kingdom according to Galatians 5:21.

# Your Body is for God, Your Maker

> Don't you know that you yourselves are God's temple and that
> God's Spirit lives in you? If anyone destroys God's temple,
> God will destroy him; for God's temple is sacred, and you are
> that temple.                    (1 Corinthians 3:16-17 NIV)

Since our bodies are the temples of a holy God, God has given us specific guidelines and principles, laws and regulations, with regard to our sexuality. Let's look at the temple instructions God gave Ezekiel to give to the Israelites, which underscores how we are to pursue holiness through the use of our bodies. God said to Ezekiel:

> Son of man, tell the people of Israel all about the Temple so
> they'll be dismayed by their wayward lives. Get them to go
> over the layout. That will bring them up short. Show them the
> whole plan of the Temple, its ins and outs, the proportions, the
> regulations, and the laws. Draw a picture so they can see the
> design and meaning and live by its design and intent. "This
> is the law of the Temple: As it radiates from the top of the
> mountain, everything around it becomes holy ground. Yes, this
> is law, the meaning, of the Temple.    (Ezekiel 43:10-12 MSG)

In this book, I point out from the Bible some of the intents of our bodies, and sexuality as envisioned by our heavenly Father, the Creator of the universe. The human body houses our spirit, which embodies the image of God in man. As Christians, we are reminded in 1 Peter 2:5 that God is building us as living stones into His spiritual temple. In the end, we become His holy priesthood to offer spiritual sacrifices, pleasing to Him through our Lord Jesus Christ. We are therefore to present our bodies as a living sacrifice. Paul under the inspiration of the Holy Spirit wrote:

> I APPEAL to you therefore, brethren, and beg of you in view
> of [all] the mercies of God, to make a decisive dedication of
> your bodies [presenting all your members and faculties] as a
> living sacrifice, holy (devoted, consecrated) and well pleasing
> to God, which is your reasonable (rational, intelligent) service
> and spiritual worship.                    (Romans 12:1 AMP)

Our bodies are not to be used as instruments of sexual immorality to displease the Spirit of God in us. Most people are unable to see the body as the spiritual temple for God; therefore, they do not see the rationale to offer it as a living sacrifice, pleasing to Him. The devil likes to counterfeit anything God does. If you allow evil spirits to possess your gate, they can erect a spiritual altar in you to destroy your body. Your body is not yours to do with as you please. It belongs to God. Don't abuse it and don't lend it out to the devil. He is already doomed. Whatever he touches breeds nothing, but death.

Just as God uses man to accomplish His purposes on earth, so does the devil, who currently has the world systems under his dominion. As a Christian, and a pilgrim in this world, you are warned not to:

> Become so well-adjusted to your culture that you fit into it without even thinking. Instead, fix your attention on God. You'll be changed from the inside out. Readily recognize what he wants from you, and quickly respond to it. Unlike the culture around you, always dragging you down to its level of immaturity, God brings the best out of you, develops well-formed maturity in you.                 (Romans 12:2 MSG)

We live in an age where sexual promiscuity is at its highest. The almighty God has placed in every society the concepts of sexual taboos concerning virginity, chastity, abstinence, and monogamy as guidelines for family and marriage. However, over the years, these have been downgraded and relegated to the backseat of our sexuality and relationships. Have you ever wondered why? The Bible warns us not abuse our bodies but rather to elevate the standard of sexual purity befitting God's chosen people.

> You know the guidelines we laid out for you from the Master Jesus. God wants you to live a pure life. Keep yourselves from sexual promiscuity. Learn to appreciate and give dignity to your body, not abusing it, as is so common among those who know nothing of God.              (1 Thessalonians 4:2-5 MSG)

Over the centuries, renaissance thinkers and philosophers have said that people don't need God and that we can do better by ourselves.

Human secularism stresses individual dignity, worth, and capacity for self-realization through reason to achieve one's dreams, not through some dogmas of organized religion or spirituality. Can a man pull himself up by his own bootstraps? Yet this is precisely what human secularism advocates. Be careful of those who use the word *empowerment* loosely. What is the source of this power? True empowerment is spiritual and divine, not physical. When it comes to sexuality, loose moral concepts lead to loose attitudes and sexual promiscuity.

## Indecent Proposal

On September 17, 2004, I was listening to a program *Love, Lust & Lies*, on a New York City radio station (KISSfm 98.7), testing the pulse of its listeners concerning the movie *Indecent Proposal.* Callers to the station were asked if they would allow their mates to "sleep" with another person for one million dollars.

Some said they would, and others said, "no way." One woman said, "Why not have sex for a million dollars when the men are sleeping around anyway, without bringing home any money?" This makes a lot of sense philosophically. A million dollars can accomplish much. After all, even the Bible says money is a defense (Ecclesiastes 7:12). But beware of the adages "All that glitters is not gold" and "Money can't buy happiness." Where a couple is in a bind, I can understand the rationale for wanting the money because of some dire consequences beyond their control. There may even be life-and-death scenarios whereby the money could be used to save the life of a partner, or a loved one. But is the saving of physical life, always preferred over death? Is physical life to be chosen over spiritual life?

The case against going for the million dollars may not appeal to many in an age where marriage is viewed as an economic union. However, there are many hidden dangers. First, there is a possibility that the spouse who went in for the sex may contract an STD. A million dollars will not buy back the life of its victim. Second, sleeping with someone unites the souls of the individuals involved, not to mention inviting evil spirits to violate the life of an unsuspecting victim. Whenever you sell your body for money, you have in essence sold your soul to the devil. Your spiritual captors will tighten your yoke. Some virtues in you would die that day, to be replaced with demons of confusion, shame, regret, humiliation, depression, and degradation, which would make you feel very cheap.

The male ego may sound and act tough, but it is very fragile. It can easily be bruised. On the surface, everything may look good, but deep down there could be a lingering suspicion that his woman is cheating on him. This will undermine the relationship. The male ego cannot stand to see his woman in the arms of another man. If this problem is not dealt with right away, it can bring the relationship to ruins. The male ego cannot be bought by money where true love for his woman is concerned. Money is but half the solution to marital problems or else there will be no divorce among rich folks.

Money is not evil per se, but the love of money is. It competes for attention. It will demand its dues. Hear the words of our Lord Jesus:

> No one can serve two masters; for either he will hate the one and love the other, or he will stand by and be devoted to the one and despise and be against the other. You cannot serve God and mammon (deceitful riches, money, possessions, or whatever is trusted in).                    (Matthew 6:24 AMP)

> Labour not to be rich: cease from thine own wisdom. Wilt thou set thine eyes upon that which is not? For riches certainly make themselves wings; they fly away as an eagle toward heaven.
>                          (Proverbs 23:4-5)

We live in a humanistic society, where the supernatural is rejected in favor of an individual's dignity and worth to make decisions based on his intellectual capacity to reason. We have wholeheartedly embraced sexual existentialism, which encourages people to assume ultimate responsibility for what they do with their bodies, without anybody dictating to them what is right or wrong, good or bad. As a result, we have failed to realize the divine purpose of our existence, and in the process, have neglected to honor God by doing what we please with our bodies. Don't wait until the latter end of your life, to find out what was required of you.

> Remember now thy Creator in the days of thy youth, while the evil days come not, nor the years draw nigh, when thou shalt say, I have no pleasure in them; Let us hear the conclusion of the whole matter: Fear God, and keep his commandments: for this is the whole duty of man. For God shall bring every work into judgment, with every secret thing, whether it be good, or whether it be evil.
>
> (Ecclesiastes 12:1, 13-14)

## Sexual Revolution of the 1960s

In the 1960s, traditionalist views of our sexuality were thrown into turmoil as the baby boomers of the post-war era sought to overthrow the conservative views of the 1950s. The sexual revolution exploded, changing the cultural fabric of the American society. In America, earlier changes, such as the separation of church and state, laid the foundation for today's Libertarian views to displace the puritan moral codes of sexuality, which were deemed to be too restrictive and suppressive. In a sense, the hedonistic secularism of the sexual revolution of the 1960s demanded that people be allowed the freedom to indulge in their sexuality by aligning their dust nature (or "survival instinct," the term favored by psychologists and social anthropologists) with that of the animal kingdom, without any interference from the government or society at large, all in the name of "love." Love? Beware, erotic lust can be a powerful delirium.

The perceived notion that the church has suppressed sex for so long, combined with the fact that the churches have been telling people to put their libidos in check without telling them the full spiritual "whys," may have caused people to rebel or take lightly teachings linking sexuality and its spiritual ramifications. I believe the lack of knowledge in the area of spiritual matters (specifically, spiritual warfare teachings), and the reluctancy of mainstream churches to talk about demons and Satan for fear of glorifying him, has made people less fearful of violating spiritual laws concerning our sexuality.

In the end, anything spiritual that encroached on our freedom to indulge in our sensuality or to gratify the flesh was deemed superstitious and was therefore rendered superfluous by reason, logic, and scientific research. A "new morality" emerged, which swung the pendulum from one perceived extreme of sexual suppression to the other extreme of unrestricted sexual freedom. The churches were not ready to deal with the proliferation of sexual promiscuity and havoc that was about to descend on our generation. The resultant "sexual revolution" led to increased casual sex, teen sex, pregnant teens, unwed mothers and fathers, pornography, singles bars, one-night stands, group sex, swingers, divorces, open marriages, cohabitation, rape, incest, abortions, alternate sexual preferences, sexual abuse, and STDs such as AIDS.

What was once considered shameful has now become acceptable. Nowadays, it is politically correct to water down sexual perversions as "personal sexual preferences" and for people to use terminology such as "significant other" and "satellite relationships" when talking about illicit sexual affairs. They camouflage sexual deviancy in scientific and socio-psychological expressions, instead of calling it by its real name: sin (i.e.; to miss the mark). The cumulative effect on the quality of family life is evidenced by higher divorce rates, broken homes, troubled youths, premarital sex, prostitution, teen pregnancies, abortions, and sexually transmitted disease,--a high price that society pays for neglecting its communal responsibilities.

When people come under demonic attacks because of lack of spiritual knowledge, they seek physical solutions and look to psychotherapists or other counselors for help. Yet such nonspiritual sources don't help, and may eventually make matters worse. A spiritual cure can only be achieved by faith, through prayers and fasting.

In conjunction with counseling, others seek medical remedies for their emotional and mental problems. Yet if a person's psychiatric problem is spiritual, no amount of antidepressant or medication can cure or save that person. At best, it will only alleviate the symptoms. Recently, the US government warned the public about a link between antidepressant drugs and suicide in teens.

When the disciples of Jesus could not cure a person with a dumb and deaf spirit, Jesus said to them, "This kind can come forth by nothing, but by prayer and fasting" (Mark 9:29). In prayer and fasting, you humble yourself, and seek divine help to intervene in your situation. However, these are only effective if you are obedient to God's commandments. Be careful of your sex life.

## Don't Violate Spiritual Laws Concerning Sexuality

God created everything in the universe for a purpose. He set laws and commandments to sustain, and maintain His creation. Therefore, we need to observe established patterns of sexual purity as He has ordained. God did not intend for us to have multiple sexual partners.

> To avoid fornication, let every man have his own wife, and let every woman have her own husband.     (1 Corinthians 7:2)

All human beings live by rules and are guided by laws, be they religious, moral, social, or political. Violating these laws has ramifications. When we transgress spiritual sexual laws in the Bible, there will be punishment. When a land is defiled, God says: "I do visit the iniquity thereof upon it, and the land itself vomiteth out her inhabitants" (Leviticus 18:25).

People who don't know or care about the God of the Bible, the one who created heaven and earth, are no different from the Pharaoh who said: "Who is the LORD, that I should obey his voice to let Israel go? I know not the LORD, neither will I let Israel go" (Exodus 5:2). Eventually, Pharaoh freed the Israelites, at the cost of his firstborn.

> The Israelites set out from Rameses on the fifteenth day of the first month, the day after the Passover. They marched out boldly in full view of all the Egyptians, who were burying all their firstborn, whom the LORD had struck down among them; for the LORD had brought judgment on their gods.
> (Numbers 33:3-4 NIV)

Prior to the 1960s, gonorrhea and syphilis were among the prevailing STDs. Then came viral genital herpes, a more troublesome STD than gonorrhea. In the 1980s came a disease called HIV/AIDS, which has killed a lot of people mostly, caused by people whose partners had engaged in illicit sexual activities.

I believe that eventually, AIDS will be cured or contained, just like herpes. However, violating spiritual laws of sexuality will always have devastating consequences even for generations to come.

For a believer of Jesus Christ, your body is the temple of the Holy Spirit. Don't abuse it. Don't defile it sexually, or you may pay a high price. Our bodies are to be used in the service of our Creator. Are you overweight (your health is at risk), addicted to drugs, alcohol, sex, pornography, cigarette, or even food? Are you dabbling in the occult, Eastern mysticism and other secret societies, do you consult psychics, are you a member of any false religion, do you study yoga?

Today, people become spiritually impotent when they open themselves up to demonic influences by following fashion blindly, such as piercing and tattooing their bodies, men braiding their hair, wearing earrings, and doing things that are in violation of their sexuality. My main concern is people who dress in a transgendered manner (the gender-benders). If you think there is no harm done, hear what God says about tattooing:

> Ye shall not make any cuttings in your flesh for the dead, nor print any marks upon you: I am the LORD. (Leviticus 19:28)

> Having therefore these promises, dearly beloved, let us cleanse ourselves from all filthiness of the flesh and spirit, perfecting holiness in the fear of God. (2 Corinthians 7:1)

Christians have been redeemed at a great price. We are to glorify God in our bodies and our spirits because we belong to God. A sexually defiled person cannot offer his body as a "living sacrifice," holy and pleasing to God, in fulfillment of his spiritual worship.

## Sexual Immorality and Demonic Infestations

Have you ever wondered why sexual temptations are so hard to resist? Sexual sins are pleasurable. Without the enjoyment in sex, procreation would have become a chore. But as you enjoy yourself in the physical, spiritually, you may be wasting away in death.

Some people equate sex with love and so they see no harm in expressing themselves sexually. Moreover, how can something as pleasurable as sex between two consenting adults be wrong? The Bible contains many references to maintain our sexual purity. Sex was designed to be enjoyed within the parameters of marriage, not with multiple partners, and definitely not with evil spirits or demons. These commandments are not from a "killjoy" God who does not want us to enjoy sex. On the contrary, the commandments are, first of all, to help us avoid demonic infestations. Evil spirits can put us in bondage, to steal, kill, and destroy our blessings and our lives. Our God is a holy God. Without holiness we become unclean and defiled, and cannot fellowship with Him. Your body has a spiritual purpose; to be used in God's service. Don't lend it to the devil.

In ancient Babylon and in some pagan religions, temple prostitutes were used as conduits by which demons and evil spirits were passed on to unsuspecting clients. Rape and violent sexual molestation of children have been known to open doorways to some powerful and wicked demons. These demons will invade and violate a person whenever the opportunity presents itself. Sometimes they prefer children, who are vulnerable, so they can tag along for the longest ride, to use their bodies for their vile, and evil escapades. In the end, these evil spirits discard their victims after they have destroyed them, and move on to the next person.

For adults, any involvement in sado-masochistic sex, or sexual perversion, causes the infestation of powerful demons that can cause a man to become serial rapist. Look at the life of a serial killer or a hardcore prostitute, or even porn artist who performs live sex on stage. The first time it is tough on them, but thereafter it becomes a piece of cake. Why is this the case? We all have gates or doors to our spirits. If your gate is conquered, a spirit of greediness, or lust may open the door and invite spirits such as pride of sexual power, pride of body, spirit of hard-heartedness, violence, fantasy, and other vile spirits to come in. As more demons enter, powerful and wicked spirits also take up residency in the individual. In the end, something that started out as so benign or innocent, leads to spiritual captivity and tragedy.

The serial killer will therefore murder in cold blood without qualms. The hardcore porn artist would perform degradable live sexual acts on stage for money without shame. After they have been used and are no longer needed, they are sold to the spirit of heaviness such as deep hurt, self-pity, hatred, depression, resentment, and finally, even suicide to torment the souls of these individuals. Since these problems are spiritually induced, when it comes to rehabilitation, no amount of psychological counseling can save these individuals, only divine intervention can set them free. If you know of people who are caught up in the devil's web, have hope; even a simple prayer offered in faith, could trigger their deliverance. Our God is merciful. In the day of trouble call Him as written, " 'In that day,' declares the LORD Almighty, 'I will break the yoke off their necks and will tear off their bonds; no longer will foreigners enslave them." (Jeremiah 30:8.)

## No One is Immune from Demonic Attack

Men of God should refrain from flirting with women in their congregations. I was talking to a visiting pastor in our church in the Bronx, New York, when the topic of pastors who become involved in sexual improprieties came up. He told me the following.

During one ministration service the pastor, under the unction of the Holy Spirit, spoke out, "There is an agent here who is from the sea; that person should come forward." A beautiful woman got up and came to the front and confessed that there were twenty human agents of a mermaid spirit from the sea, beautiful ladies sent to seduce the men of God. Any man who had sex with one of them had marine spirits planted in him. This man would then be attracted to any woman with a marine spirit, to have sex with her. Eventually, any anointing, or fire of God in him would be doused.

Another problem area is with male pastors counseling female members concerning sexual problems. A witch can easily throw a demon of lust at the pastor. Pastors should always have another female member present during any counseling. Satan can use counseling of the opposite sex to trap a pastor. Men of God are not immune from sexual attacks. Even pastors can fall from grace when they play with fire by testing their sexual willpower.

Paul urges older women to counsel the younger ones in the congregation. The pastor should never take it upon himself alone to counsel female members who may be going through marital problems. Violation of this principle can lead to an unpleasant, shameful, and disastrous situation for the church. No one is immune from sexual temptation; that is why the Bible admonishes us to stay vigilant and pray continually.

There is nothing in the Bible without meaning and purpose. If you study and meditate on God's law book, the blueprint for your life, you will understand why we are to refrain from doing certain things, that are traps set by the devil to ensnare us due to our ignorance of spiritual matters.

## Avoid Spiritual Quick Fixes

A friend of mine recounted the story of a lady who had problems sustaining long-term relationships with potential mates. She confided in a friend, who then took her to see a "juju" (voodoo) man. This man had the lady open her legs, and a reptile was allowed to lick between her thighs.

After some time went by, this lady met a disheveled man, literally a madman, who beckoned to her. She found herself following this stranger to an empty lot, where he raped her. She couldn't find the courage to tell anyone at the time.

Some of the missing-persons stories are rooted in instances where children were charmed into following their kidnapers and perpetrators. Some of these children became victims of ritualistic sexual molestation or ended up as human sacrifices on satanic altars.

When the reptile made contact with that lady demons were transferred into her. In fact, there are many ways through which evil spirits gain access to keep us in bondage, harm us, or influence our behavior. When these evil squatters are present, you always find yourself doing the wrong thing, in contrary to the will of God.

Once inside the woman, certain spirits prefer different locations of the body. Some serpentine spirits tend to reside in the female genitalia and reproductive organs. I shudder to think anyone kissing, or licking a serpentine spirit! Do you want your spirit to be intertwined with a serpentine spirit? I hope not! During deliverance ministrations, when these spirits manifest in their victims, the women often crawl on the floor like a snake. It is not a pretty sight!

In deliverance session, a victim normally acts out the traits, and characteristics of the demon in them. For those with a marine spirit, the women shiver like a fish out of water. An alcoholic would act drunk and wasted. Those plagued with spiritual marriage cannot stand still on their feet, and sway from side to side. A homosexual would have a smirk of lust on his face, and a person being stalked by the spirit of death would slump to the floor as if dead. A birdlike spirit would act as if it were taking off. An angry, stubborn, or coward spirit would manifest itself in the demeanor of its victim. Have you ever wondered why some people look and act so strange? You may find your answer in the realm of the spirit.

When I was first introduced to the deliverance ministry, these strange occurrences were new to me, so I videotaped some of them. But after a while, I stopped because they became routine. Besides, I had seen enough and read of several similar accounts from other prominent deliverance ministry workers such as Derek Prince, and Dr. Rebecca Brown. It is up to me to wisely apply the knowledge I have acquired to glorify God.

## Solomon's Delight

One of the things I find puzzling about Solomon is why he didn't apply his wisdom to heed the warning God gave him to stay away from foreign women, whom the Lord had said would bring his downfall. We read:

> King Solomon, however, loved many foreign women besides Pharaoh's daughter--Moabites, Ammonites, Edomites, Sidonians and Hittites. They were from nations about which the LORD had told the Israelites, "You must not intermarry with them, because they will surely turn your hearts after their gods."
>
> Nevertheless, Solomon held fast to them in love. He had seven hundred wives of royal birth and three hundred concubines, and his wives led him astray.
>
> As Solomon grew old, his wives turned his heart after other gods, and his heart was not fully devoted to the LORD his God, as the heart of David his father had been. He followed Ashtoreth the goddess of the Sidonians, and Molech the detestable god of the Ammonites. So Solomon did evil in the eyes of the LORD; he did not follow the LORD completely, as David his father had done.          (1 Kings 11:1-6 NIV)

Although God had given Solomon the name "Jedidiah" (beloved of the Lord) (2 Samuel 12:25), he chose to love pagan women, in defiance of God's covenant with him. There are two conclusions that come to mind. The first is that God gave Solomon wisdom, but did not interfere with his free will, his freedom of choice in how to apply it. The second is that because of his wisdom, Solomon perhaps became complacent and took the mercies of God for granted.

He ended up worshiping the gods of these heathen women. Here is divine revelation; according to Jeremiah 50:7, when you have unconfessed sins in your life, you give the enemy legal grounds to attack and overpower you. There is no doubt in my mind that his association, and having sex with these women, opened Solomon up to some powerful demons of lust, pride, and complacency, which made him very susceptible, not only to follow these women but also to worship their gods, and thereby losing some of his anointing.

In the end, God punished King Solomon, for his disobedience and illicit sexual escapades, in violation of His commandments. In the book of 1 Kings we read:

> The LORD became angry with Solomon because his heart had turned away from the LORD, the God of Israel, who had appeared to him twice. Although he had forbidden Solomon to follow other gods, Solomon did not keep the LORD's command.
>
> So the LORD said to Solomon, "Since this is your attitude and you have not kept my covenant and my decrees, which I commanded you, I will most certainly tear the kingdom away from you and give it to one of your subordinates. Nevertheless, for the sake of David your father, I will not do it during your lifetime. I will tear it out of the hand of your son."
>
> (1 Kings 11: 9-12 NIV)

We are all responsible for our actions, and will definitely reap what we sow. Toward the end of his life, Solomon became unprofitable. He even tried to kill the person whom God had anointed to rule in his stead.

Most of us are no different from King Solomon. We know the Ten Commandments, we know what is right, yet we choose to sin. We deliberately disobey our conscience, the inner voice that tells us, "Don't go there; don't look; don't touch, don't do that." If we are not careful, the spirit of lust will inflame our passions and desires, to betray and ensnare us. God will not interfere with our natural urges. Outer beauty without inner godly virtues can become a double-edged sword to harm us. It is our obligation to rein in our libidos, and keep our sexual urges in check. You know your weaknesses pray to stay away from them.

God commands us to practice sexual purity, not only because He is holy, but also as a way of protecting us from demonic infestation. When God calls you, first He prepares you before He commissions you. God cannot use you if you are full of pride with an unrepentant heart. If you are sexually defiled He will purge you. He will put you through fire to refine you. Your preparation period may entail suffering (baptism by fire). Sometimes, it is during this period that the devil cannot resist and steps in to help with your preparation.

For a Christian, it is okay to have doubts at times because you don't understand or see the whole picture as God deals with your situation. But to those who keep asking, "If God is good, why is there so much suffering in the world?" be reminded that not every suffering is bad per se. Listen to James:

> Consider it wholly joyful, my brethren, whenever you are enveloped in or encounter trials of any sort or fall into various temptations. Be assured and understand that the trial and proving of your faith bring out endurance and steadfastness and patience.
>
> But let endurance and steadfastness and patience have full play and do a thorough work, so that you may be [people] perfectly and fully developed [with no defects], lacking in nothing.
> (James 1:2-4 AMP)

## Are People Born with Sexual Aberration?

Can people be born transgendered or homosexual? The Bible tells us that there is nothing new under the sun. In ancient days, cross-dressing, and the transgender phenomenon just like homosexuality, were hot polarizing issues that affected society. I'm sure there were those who sought to legitimize these practices. But this is what the Prophet Isaiah wrote concerning such an issue:

> [Oh, your perversity!] You turn things upside down! Shall the potter be considered of no more account than the clay? Shall

> the thing that is made say of its maker, He did not make me; or
> the thing that is formed say of him who formed it, He has no
> understanding?                                    (Isaiah 29:16 AMP)

Some view homosexuality as a lifestyle of sexual preference, others think it's all about genetics, something you're born with. But there is a popular saying that, *"God never makes junk."* In the beginning God created male and female, Adam and Eve. There was no confusion among the sexes. Who or what is responsible for this confusion? Spiritual forces have exerted enormous influences in the lives of men, and women to cause the confusion we see in society. Homosexuality, and transgender have a lot more to do with spirituality than sexuality.

Later we shall look at some of the ways the devil attempts to divide, weaken, and destroy the institution of marriage, and family.

## Help Me! I'm Becoming Transgendered

Of late you see on TV people talking about being trapped in the wrong body. Why the intense desire for a different body? I watched a show on transgender (Born in the Wrong Body-The 11-year-old who wants a sex change) and was saddened by the fact that the spiritual implications of the phenomenon were not explored. In the book of Isaiah we are warned; "Woe to him who quarrels with his Maker" (Isaiah 45:9). To those who have finally gone ahead, and performed sex change to be at peace with their sexuality, be warned:

> But who are you, O man, to talk back to God? "Shall what is
> formed say to him who formed it, 'Why did you make me like
> this?' Does not the potter have the right to make out of the
> same lump of clay some pottery for noble purposes and some
> for common use?"                                (Romans 9:20-21 NIV)

Oprah interviewed the parents of a five-year-old boy who was exhibiting signs and symptoms of childhood abnormality. At first, the father was distraught at what was happening to his child. But at the end of the show, he chose to accept the apparent futility of his son's situation and gave up the fight for the sanctity of his child's sexuality. Why? He took consolation in another person's situation, a guy who had been married and, after having fathered four kids, decided to come clean as a transvestite.

Apparently the producers of the show were unaware of the connection between spirituality and sexuality. Or perhaps it was politically correct to avoid the issue of spirituality in an age of blurred sexuality. I'm inclined to give Oprah the benefit of the doubt because she is not known to shy away from controversy. Homosexuality is an ugly spirit that wages war against the minds and bodies of its victims to defile, and destroy them.

Homosexuals talk about their intense attraction and desire to be with another man. If that was the only problem, I could live with that. Having an intense desire for something is one thing, we all do; but acting on your impulses is another. Listen to what Paul says about something within us that pushes us to do wrong and undesirable things.

> For I endorse and delight in the Law of God in my inmost self
> [with my new nature]. But I discern in my bodily members in
> the sensitive appetites and wills of the flesh] a different law
> (rule of action) at war against the law of my mind (my reason)
> and making me a prisoner to the law of sin that dwells in my
> bodily organs in the sensitive appetites and wills of the flesh].
> O unhappy and pitiable and wretched man that I am! Who will
> release and deliver me from [the shackles of] this body of death?
> (Romans 7:22-24 AMP)

According to Romans 6:16, what you choose to obey becomes your master, either of sin to death, or to God which leads to righteousness.

But the unspiritual considers the desires of the heart an individual sexual preferences, or a private right. Do private matters outweigh the need of society to perpetuate itself? Is there an inherent good in homosexuality, and does it have a role to play in today's society?

*The World History of Male Love: The Androphile Project* is a chronicle of same-sex love, particularly male love, over the course of history. The project points out what it calls: "The big lie that same-sex love is 'against nature,' a fiction which flies in the face of both biology and history, [and] depends on censorship for its survival." *(Androphile Gay History Project: The World History of male Love.)*

## The Androphile Project

According to the researchers of the project, the aim of the Androphile Project is to "undo that censorship by publicizing gay love's role in man's spirit and culture: to document its successes, its failures, and the controversies it has encountered over the course of human history."

The project points to biological studies (by Levay, 1994; Reinisch, et al., 1991) documenting the differences between male homosexuals and heterosexuals in their exposure to prenatal hormones, possibly linking them to testosterone exposure (Jamison, et al., 1993). They also pointed to a study by Zucker, et al. (1993) and a similar study by Green (1987), which found out that parents of girlish-looking (effeminate) boys judged their babies more "beautiful" babies than other children.

The above studies sought to establish a genetic basis for the perpetuation of homosexuality in our society, a biological phenomenon, and therefore not anti-nature. The project also attempts to legitimize and lend credence to same-sex intercourse as a necessary social behavior. It maintains that evidence of same-sex love has been quietly suppressed or censored, resulting in a deception that has needlessly polarize society into "untold suffering for those people who happen to fall in love with others of their own sex." Why are some males attracted to boys and men so much that they crave to unleash their male eros in a sexual act? The fact that someone is handsome does not mean the person should be looked upon as a sex object. This is sexual perversion and an abomination.

Pushed to its logical conclusion, the human race could be extinct if everybody became homosexual. This is anti-nature and an aberration in the plans of the Creator, who created male and female, and gave them the mandate to multiply and subdue the earth. Same-sex sexual intercourse is a taboo and a curse of our sexuality, no matter how you view it. Homosexuality is more than a lifestyle; it is a spiritual snare to those caught in its trap with men lusting after men, in an evil spiritual union. The Androphile Project also seeks to lend weight to the debate on gay marriages, which it claims has been "a tradition documented the world over for thousands of years, but nowhere as widely or as recently as in North America."

With same-sex marriage, how are children to be procreated? Who do they expect to be surrogate mothers? This brings to mind the current phenomenon called "Down Low" (hidden sexual lifestyle of husbands sleeping with other men), which apparently is not new. It is well documented in history, particularly in the city-states of ancient Greece and Rome, where people stayed in a married relationship, but also satisfied their male eros for same-sex cravings on the side.

The Androphile Project points to the likes of Alexander the Great and his boyfriend, Hephaestion, and the Japanese, shogun who, besides his concubines, had many male companions. Then there were the "tobiko" (traveling young kabuki actors) who, during the day, would put on a brilliant stage performance to please their audiences, and at night participate in homosexual acts to please their customers.

Same–sex love may be on the rise, but it is in the minority. However, society will still suffer the consequences of a perverted generation when the wrath of God is unleashed upon the land. Deep down in the heart of these men, they know there is a God, but they have refused to acknowledge Him. As a result, there is a curse on the hearts of sexual deviants, and the children of the disobedient for making God's truth a lie. We read:

> For the wrath of God is revealed from heaven against all
> ungodliness and unrighteousness of men, who hold the truth in
> unrighteousness; Because that which may be known of God is

manifest in them; for God hath shewed it unto them.

For the invisible things of him from the creation of the world are clearly seen, being understood by the things that are made, even his eternal power and Godhead; so that they are without excuse: Because that, when they knew God, they glorified him not as God, neither were thankful; but became vain in their imaginations, and their foolish heart was darkened.

Professing themselves to be wise, they became fools, And changed the glory of the uncorruptible God into an image made like to corruptible man, and to birds, and fourfooted beasts, and creeping things.

Wherefore God also gave them up to uncleanness through the lusts of their own hearts, to dishonour their own bodies between themselves: Who changed the truth of God into a lie, and worshipped and served the creature more than the Creator, who is blessed forever. Amen.

For this cause God gave them up unto vile affections: for even their women did change the natural use into that which is against nature:

And likewise also the men, leaving the natural use of the woman, burned in their lust one toward another; men with men working that which is unseemly, and receiving in themselves that recompence of their error which was meet.

And even as they did not like to retain God in their knowledge, God gave them over to a reprobate mind, to do those things which are not convenient;

Being filled with all unrighteousness, fornication, wickedness, covetousness, maliciousness; full of envy, murder, debate, deceit, malignity; whisperers, Backbiters, haters of God, despiteful, proud, boasters, inventors of evil things, disobedient to parents. Without understanding, covenant breakers, without natural affection, implacable, unmerciful: Who knowing the judgment of God, that they which commit such things are worthy of death, not only do the same, but have pleasure in them that do them." (Romans 1:18-32)

Ironically, the Androphile Project does not mention the destruction of Sodom and Gomorrah for their homosexual practices and other sexual perversions and wickedness. Purity is a life and death issue.

## Teach the Children Sexual Purity

When it comes to our children, how quick are we to exonerate them when the ax of morality falls too close to home. How would you feel if a judge, on the Supreme Court decides to tweak the law in favor of a child caught up in immorality because his or her child would be denied certain rights and therefore be seen as second-class citizen? I am referring particularly to gay marriages. Marriage has never been defined as a union between same sex love. Homosexuality is anti-creation, in direct violation of the divine will and command for male and female to multiply, and fill (subdue) the earth.

Your love and support for your child does not mean you should condone sin, rather seek help for your loved one. If you are a Christian go to the throne room of grace, to the mercy seat and let your request made known to God. Enlist the help of Jesus, who stands at the Right hand side of the Father to intercede on your behalf. Each man will suffer for his actions, or for his part no matter how small it is. Ignorance is no accuse:

> That servant who knows his master's will and does not get ready or does not do what his master wants will be beaten with many blows. But the one who does not know and does things deserving punishment will be beaten with few blows. From everyone who has been given much, much will be demanded; and from the one who has been entrusted with much, much more will be asked. (Luke 12:47-48 NIV)

For those who are sympathetic to the course of same sex love, and indirectly help to propagate gay lifestyle, you do so in direct violation of God's commandment not to be unequally yoked to an unbeliever. You also risk inviting the spirit of homosexuality to ensnare your family.

The devil needs human agents to execute and fulfill his grand designs.

The devil is not stupid; he knows where to get fresh supplies. Demons in the earthly realm like to indwell humans, and so what better place to start looking than our vulnerable children? They want to start with them right from the womb, to be part of their growth process. So when parents neglect to take care of their kids spiritually, they step in to plant the seed of destruction in their lives.

If a pedophile were to put a gun to a child's head and molest him, the whole society will be in uproar and appalled. They should be because that is a heinous crime. But let's consider a situation where a straight family invites a gay couple to their home because they are seen as successful, wealthy, happy and in love with each other. With children in the home, sooner or later the children will become desensitized to the gay lifestyle and begin to believe that it is an alternative viable option. God forbid, should they ever be jilted in their quest for love and intimacy and decided to try same sex love which they see as harmless, what would you do? Nobody put a gun to their heads, you did. You are responsible to teach spiritual truths to your children and help them put boundaries to their sexuality.

Illicit sexual intercourse is one of the many ways to pass demons from one person to another. One miserable lousy sexual encounter could be your undoing. You could become the sex slave of a mean, slimy, filthy spirit. All of your children will belong to that spirit to do with as it pleases including selling them to other spirits, such as disappointment, failure, fear, anxiety, chronic disease, depression, and suicidal thoughts. Remember, some of today's children will grow up to become tomorrow's child molesters, pedophiles, porn artists, and so forth.

Today, social scientists make every effort to psychoanalyze the impact of sexual deviancy, but neglect to see the spiritual dimension of the problem. Just because the spiritual, cannot be seen with the naked eye does not mean it will not harm you if you violate any spiritual rules.

There is a big spiritual warfare impacting the sanctity of the marriage institution, and the family structure. Be proactive and teach your children sexual purity, before the entertainment media teaches them sexual deviancy. Sexual practices that were considered taboo in the past are no longer off limits, even to our children. The battle for your child's sexual purity must first start in the realm of the spirit, because the spiritual supersedes the physical. Satan is spiritual, and so you lose the war when you try to fight evil in the physical. That is why the Bible reminds us that we are engaged in spiritual warfare, the weapon we fight with is not of the world, or flesh and blood, but of God's divine power, which alone is capable of pulling down and demolishing the devil's strongholds in our lives. The physical war of your family must therefore, first be won spiritually.

God cautioned the ancient Israelites not to engage in any of the abominable sexual practices in the land to which He was sending them. His laws were not only meant for the adults, but also for the children, and their descendants. Moses commanded the Israelites:

> Love the LORD your God with all your heart and with all your soul and with all your strength. These commandments that I give you today are to be upon your hearts. Impress them on your children.
>
> Talk about them when you sit at home and when you walk along the road, when you lie down and when you get up. Tie them as symbols on your hands and bind them on your foreheads. Write them on the doorframes of your houses and on your gates.
>
> And what other nation is so great as to have such righteous decrees and laws as this body of laws I am setting before you today? Only be careful, and watch yourselves closely so that you do not forget the things your eyes have seen or let them slip from your heart as long as you live. Teach them to your children and to their children after them.
>
> (Deuteronomy 6:5-9; 4:8-9)

Sexual immoralities are linked to many social problems, including abortion, which spiritually, is tantamount to offering our sons and daughters as sacrifices to Satan. It is reported that over twenty-four million abortions are performed worldwide each year. You must teach your children chastity and abstinence, or you will be accessories to murder in the event you condoned abortion. God will hold you accountable when you neglect to teach them spiritual truths and principles.

Parents who refuse to teach their children concerning sexual purity are neglecting their responsibility to their children, and giving others the opportunity to influence them, perhaps for the worse. Those who disobey God's laws come under a curse. Any disobedience in our lives can rob us of the enjoyment of our children.

> Thou shall beget sons and daughters, but thou shalt not enjoy them; for they shall go into captivity.    (Deuteronomy 28:41)

Our children can get into drugs and other socially unacceptable practices. The spirit of lust, fornication and adultery, divorce, greed, and unforgiveness can easily invade your community, no matter how affluent it is. Despite your wealth, these deviant spirits can invite other evil spirits to enter into any of the neighborhood kids to introduce your child to the occult, drugs, alcoholism, pornography, prostitution, homosexuality, and other despicable social vises that will break your heart.

Recently, a major chain store in New Jersey sent out a memo to store managers not to stop mothers from allowing their sons into the ladies' restrooms. Pedophiles had been trying to lure boys with money to have sexual relations with them in the men's restrooms, telling them that same-sex love is just as good as with the opposite sex. The pedophiles have moved their enticements into cyberspace via internet.

Nowadays, technology, and the media are being exploited for evil. Satan is saturating the world with sexual perversions to corrupt and defile many. Today's television shows, music, and entertainment are full of sexually explicit materials. Movies and videos promote sexual innuendoes, violence, and profanity in an age where shameful sexual expressions have found their way into culturally acceptable practices. The world is full of sexual lust and temptations.

77

Oprah Winfrey did a show: "Is Your Child Living a Double Life," exploring prostitution, sex, drugs, and party lifestyles of teens based on the provocative movie *Thirteen*, which depicted sexual promiscuity and other sensual aberrations among suburban teenagers. These teens came from good homes where money was not an issue, yet they were involved in social vises. How did it happen? The trouble may have started spiritually. We live in perilous times, the hour of evil temptations, as described in Revelation 3:10. A child without sexual boundaries or self-control is like a brothel offering freebees.

It is the parents' responsibility to teach their teenagers to refrain from touching and kissing before they go too far. In Proverbs we read, "He that hath no rule over his own spirit is like a city that is broken down, and without walls" (Proverbs 25:28). In these end times, if you neglect your duty to teach your children sexual moralities at an early age, the devil will. He will set them up to ruin their reputations, rob them of their youthfulness, and cause some to experience emotional, psychological and spritiual deaths.

If the devil has his way, chastity before marriage could soon become an unattainable virtue. He has put into place plans to defile children when young, impressionable, and vulnerable, creating a generation desensitized to what it means to "present your bodies as a living sacrifice, holy, acceptable unto God" as their spiritual act of worship (Roman 12:1). Open your eyes to the wider humanistic trends, such as the substitution of holy for the unholy, and lust for love.

## Demons of Peer Pressure

The devil likes to attack children, even babies. Why was baby Jesus sent to Egypt until Herod was dead before returning to Israel? Satan, represented by King Herod, had heard from the wise men that a new king had been born when they saw Jesus' star in the heavens.

When God's blessings come on the family, it can come through the father, mother, or the child. Our children are our posterity, and so instinctively we seek to protect them. The devil will attack you and your family today because he has seen your bright future. His strategy is to attack, to create confusion, to destroy, and if possible to prevent you from inheriting your destinies. How does he do it?

Humans are social beings, so we seek affection, approval, and affirmation as a society. Children are not immune from the desire for intimacy. For example, the devil knows the youth in their teenage years go through a lot of changes. They become uncertain about themselves, and may at times feel overwhelmed. Fear of rejection becomes critical. When this happens, they look for acceptance. However, anytime you envy, or compare yourself to others, the devil feeds you with insatiable appetite to cloud your senses. In their desire to fit in and be accepted, some kids try to impress, and please their peers.

It is at this point of vulnerability that the devil sets spiritual traps and sends contrary agents into their lives to lead them astray, when they succumb to peer pressure. The Bible, warns us against being yoked with the wrong crowd. We read:

> Blessed is the man that walketh not in the counsel of the ungodly, nor standeth in the way of sinners, nor sitteth in the seat of the scornful. But his delight is in the law of the LORD; and in his law doth he meditate day and night. (Psalm 1:1-2)

At the heart of our psyche is the desire to be somebody, to be accepted in both the physical as well as the realm of the spirit. But when these feelings and desires are not met, or are misplaced, they result in a yearning, a cry for intimacy with a soul mate as well as fellowship with our Maker. Some women who turned to prostitution maintain that money and other material possessions make them feel validated. However, prostitution like materialism leads to nothing but guilt, depression and further alienation.

Some have described the need for spiritual intimacy as a yearning for the ultimate "enlightenment," to be in touch with oneself and the universal consciousness. What consciousness?

As we approach the end of the age, there will be hardships and tough times on earth for everyone including children. So in times of trouble, Christians turn to the Holy Trinity for solace. They enjoy spiritual fellowship and intimacy with the triune God; God the Father (the God Head), God the Son (our Lord Jesus Christ), and God the Holy Spirit (the Spirit of God on earth),-- and with other believers, rather than be part of some universal consciousness. There is strength in numbers, and this strength comes from being in one accord spiritually. The times are evil and filled with temptations. The Bible exhorts believers not to neglect coming together.

> And let us consider how we may spur one another on toward love and good deeds. Let us not give up meeting together, as some are in the habit of doing, but let us encourage one another—and all the more as you see the Day approaching.
> (Hebrews 10:24-25)

Children, who have strong family ties and live in an environment where they are loved and accepted, are more likely to recover from emotional traumas and letdowns, than those without any support network. Teach them to avoid feasting their eyes and minds on sensual lust.

## The Snare of Pornography

According to the Bible, one of the things that defiles a man is sexual immorality. This is the only sin that directly affects our bodies, and so of all the sins, it is the one we are to flee from (1 Corinthians 6:14). Yet it is the hardest because sexual sins are so pleasurable.

We are close to the end of the age, and Satan knows his time is short. The devil's strategy is to get as many people as possible defiled, unclean, and unholy, for he knows without holiness, no one can see God. What better way to accomplish his purposes than to push to extreme the sensuality God gave for our enjoyment? He has plans for us to find pleasure in sex, no matter where we find it, how we do it, and with whom we do it, in violation of God's sexuality and purity for our lives. He wants us to disobey every sexual guideline set by our Maker and ingrained in every cultural heritage of the world. He knows that once we've been exposed to sexuality perversion, it can become an addiction. How can you recognize an addict?

You can recognize a potential sex addict by three behaviors. First, sex is his main form of interaction with others. He treats women as sex objects. Second, when he is unhappy or depressed, sex is a way of escape, the way an alcoholic would drink to avoid his problems. Finally, his behavior gets out of control, affecting family members and the community. Any addiction, whether alcoholism, drugs, lies, or sexual perversion such as pornography can lead to antisocial behavior, eventually causing divorce and family breakups.

The world of pornography has received widespread acceptance and is becoming a fabric of mainstream American culture. According to a CBS *60 Minutes* presentation on pornography, "Porn in the U.S.A," Americans spend about $10 billion a year, which is equivalent to the amount spent attending professional sporting events, buying music, or going to the movies. Consumer demand for sexually explicit materials is so strong that big companies like Marriott and Time Warner in the past made millions selling pornographic material.

In the process, many deviant sexual practices have found their way into the sacredness of matrimonial bedrooms in an attempt to spice up sex lives. Don't blindly copy new sexual experiences that are nothing but sexual exploitation motivated by greed from the adult entertainment industry.

A product that was once relegated to back alleys of big cities is now delivered into homes and hotel rooms by some of the biggest companies in the United States, according to the CBS report. All these did not happen by chance.

A spiritual force, the mystical *Babylon the Great;* the mother of all harlots is behind the push of moral decadence, and sexual deprivation. We read:

And he [angel] cried out with a mighty voice, saying, "Fallen,

fallen is Babylon the great! She has become a dwelling place of demons and a prison of every unclean spirit, and a prison of every unclean and hateful bird.

For all the nations have drunk of the wine of the passion of her immorality, and the kings of the earth have committed acts of immorality with her, and the merchants of the earth have become rich by the wealth of her sensuality."

(Revelation 18:2-3 NASB.)

Pornography distorts the wholesomeness in relationships and has contributed to the prevalence of sexual immorality and the emotional and psychological depravation that have come to characterize many broken homes.

Selling sex is one of the oldest businesses in the world, from the early temple prostitutes to today's mega-million-dollar-a-year adult entertainment industry.

According to Fred Lane, author of *Obscene Profits: The Entrepreneurs of Pornography in the Cyber Age,* the porn business is so lucrative because of the social stigma (or should I say, the desire for forbidden fruits or stolen waters) attached to sex, allowing people to charge a premium with higher profit margins.

Don't be deceived by sexual sins, because they never satisfy. Instant sensual gratification leads to nothing but the death of your relationship. To those who believe pornography is a win-win situation because it will spice up their loves lives, beware:

The end result of your perverted escapades will be death--death of your marriage, death of your financial security, death of your spiritual relationships, death of your conscience. Every person (woman, man, girl, or boy) whom you coerce into reenacting the acts you've seen in the pornographic images becomes a victim of the selfish, manipulative nature that you have as a sex/porn addict. *(Answers to tough questions. Reaching out to pornography addicts and the people who love them. Fires of Darkness Ministries. November 2004.* http://www.firesofdarkness.com).

# Individual vs. Community Rights

Some may say, "What someone does in the privacy of his bedroom is his business." But your hard-earned tax dollars pay for social services to clean up the results of messy sexual escapades. Certainly individual rights must be considered and respected by the government. But when something that starts in the privacy of people's homes can become a burden to society in the form of teen pregnancies, prostitution, abortions, unwed mothers, deadbeat dads, child molestations, STDs etc., at what point does the physical and spiritual costs to society outweigh individual rights? How do we solve the dilemma of individual versus community rights?

There are some who are milking the porn cash cow by exploiting loopholes in the laws regarding individual rights to view pornographic materials in the privacy of bedrooms. But others see pornography as a social menace, looming to come out of the bedroom and infest the community. They have mounted a counterattack to uphold community rights. This group belongs to what I call the silent majority.

Consider the issue of homosexuality. Over the ages, whenever it has reared its ugly head, it was pushed back into the closet. Now homosexuals are lobbying for national legitimacy of their practices. But the Bible, in Ephesians, warns of sensual living that can corrupt our lives and put us at odds with our Maker.

> Let no one delude and deceive you with empty excuses and groundless arguments [for these sins], for through these things the wrath of God comes upon the sons of rebellion and disobedience.
>
> So do not associate or be sharers with them. Take no part in and have no fellowship with the fruitless deeds and enterprises of darkness, but instead [let your lives be so in contrast as to] expose and reprove and convict them. For it is a shame even to speak of or mention the things that [such people] practice in secret.
>
> But when anything is exposed and reproved by the light, it is

> made visible and clear; and where everything is visible and
> clear there is light.
>
> Therefore He says, Awake, O sleeper, and arise from the dead,
> and Christ shall shine (make day dawn) upon you and give you
> light.                                   (Ephesians 5: 6-7; 11-14 AMP)

Textbooks on human sexuality contain insightful arguments by
experts and psychotherapists, pointing to some problems, which
they claim are associated with the suppression of natural sexual
urges; such as guilt, rebellion, rigidity, repression of sexual feelings,
mental illness, depression, and lack of sexual arousal or sexual
satisfaction.

Ironically, these analysts leave out behaviors that open the individual
to sexual dysfunctions and anomalies. To them, as long as sex fulfills
the pleasurable needs of the individual, even if it is at odds with the
mores of their communities, it is acceptable. However, when people
indulge in sexual practices that violate biblical rules governing our
sexuality, the ramifications can land us in trouble, including mental
health problems.

A community that allows sexual perversion to flourish will endure
the wrath of God. But God is fair, just and merciful, and so He does
not punish people without warning. He has declared that if the land
is defiled, it gets sick and so will vomit its inhabitants out.

> And if you defile the land, it will vomit you out as it vomited
> out the nations that were before you. Keep all my decrees and
> laws and follow them, so that the land where I am bringing you
> to live may not vomit you out.          (Leviticus 18:28; 20:22)
>
> If my people, which are called by my name, shall humble
> themselves, and pray, and seek my face, and turn from their
> wicked ways; then will I hear from heaven, and will forgive
> their sin, and will heal their land.          (2 Chronicles 7:14)

In the Scriptures we are encouraged to separate ourselves to avoid
punishment.

> Then I heard another voice from heaven say: "Come out of her,

my people, so that you will not share in her sins, so that you will not receive any of her plagues;    (Revelation 18:4 NIV)

What agreement [can there be between] a temple of God and idols? For we are the temple of the living God; even as God said, I will dwell in and with and among them and will walk in and with and among them, and I will be their God, and they shall be My people.

So, come out from among [unbelievers], and separate (sever) yourselves from them, says the Lord, and touch not [any] unclean thing; then I will receive you kindly and treat you with favor,

And I will be a Father to you, and you shall be My sons and daughters, says the Lord Almighty.
(2 Corinthians 6:16-18 AMP)

When people violate sexual rules, they give demons the legal grounds to invade their lives and cause all sorts of devastations, including emotional and psychological as well as medical problems such as STDs, which can lead to birth defect, and even death. Their libido may no longer respond to sexual stimuli. They may be unable to achieve orgasm; and may be unable to perform because of erectile dysfunction. These people will not be able to enjoy sex at all, and may usually end up with very low self-esteem. Here are some psychological traps of illicit sex.

1.  Worry about pregnancy, STDs and AIDS

2.  Regret

3.  Guilt

4.  Loss of self-respect and self-esteem

5.  The corruption of character and the devaluing of sex

6.  Shaken trust and fear of commitment

7.  Rage over betrayal

8.  Depression and suicide

9.  Ruined relationships

10  Stunting personal development

*http://www.stlyouth.org/reapteam/chastity/qna/hidden-traps.php-(This list was originally taken from "The Emotional Dangers of Premature Sexual Involvement" by Thomas Lickona, NAC Advisory Council Member,) (posted on abstinence.net).*

When evil spirits enter into a person, they take control and manipulate everything from biochemical balance in the brain to the physiological makeup of the individual. There is no doubt in my mind that most of the patients found in psychiatric wards need nothing but spiritual help. But who is going to set them free from bondage of mind control?

The Bible, in Proverbs 6:26-27, compares illicit sexual escapades to scooping fire to your bosom. This fire burns deep into the heart, mind, and soul. Once the fire has reached the core of your being, it begins to scorch, and rip apart your relationships by causing all sorts of emotional problems. The worldly refuse to consider spiritual options because they claim they are too subjective and unscientific. They regard absolute spirituals truths as censorship, why? They see man as the absolute definer of truth to do what he pleases.

Childhood sexual molestation is a doorway that can result in psychiatric problems, particularly those involved in ritualistic child abuses. According to Dr. Rebecca Brown (author of several books on spiritual warfare), the purpose of these rituals is to plant demons into these children, who "then exercise a profound influence on the child's growth and development, frequently almost totally controlling them." In most cases, these people suffer multiple personality disorders, or become schizophrenic. Dr. Brown maintains that the "multiple personalities" are in fact, demons. (*Prepare For War* pp. 213.) If the root cause of a person's mental problem is spiritual, no amount of antidepressants can cure him.

Only by the power of Jesus Christ can these victims of demonic infestations receive total healing. Anybody who is taking antidepressant or any psychotropic medication for emotional, and mental problems should also seek spiritual counseling and help.

## Sexual Uncleanliness

Many people have become spiritually unclean because of sexual uncleanness. They have not taken upon themselves to learn spiritual truths, and to differentiate the holy from the unclean. As a result, they have become spiritually impotent. Pornography, like other forbidden sexual practices is a spiritual contaminant. The Bible therefore urges us to discern and to avoid sexual contaminations:

> You must distinguish between the holy and the common, between the unclean and the clean.... Moreover, they shall teach My people the difference between the holy and the profane, and cause them to discern between the unclean and the clean. (Leviticus 10:10; Ezekiel 44:23 NIV)

Let us examine from the Bible some sexual practices to avoid:

> The LORD said to Moses, "Speak to the Israelites and say to them: 'I am the LORD your God. You must not do as they do in Egypt, where you used to live, and you must not do as they do in the land of Canaan, where I am bringing you. Do not follow their practices.
>
> You must obey my laws and be careful to follow my decrees. I am the LORD your God.
>
> No one is to approach any close relative to have sexual relations. I am the LORD.
>
> Do not have sexual relations with your brother's wife; that would dishonor your brother.'
>
> Do not take your wife's sister as a rival wife and have sexual relations with her while your wife is living.
>
> Do not approach a woman to have sexual relations during the uncleanness of her monthly period.
>
> Do not have sexual relations with your neighbor's wife and

defile yourself with her.

Do not lie with a man as one lies with a woman; that is detestable.

Do not have sexual relations with an animal and defile yourself with it. A woman must not present herself to an animal to have sexual relations with it; that is a perversion.

Do not defile yourselves in any of these ways, because this is how the nations that I am going to drive out before you became defiled.

Even the land was defiled; so I punished it for its sin, and the land vomited out its inhabitants. But you must keep my decrees and my laws.

The native-born and the aliens living among you must not do any of these detestable things, for all these things were done by the people who lived in the land before you, and the land became defiled.

And if you defile the land, it will vomit you out as it vomited out the nations that were before you.

Keep my requirements and do not follow any of the detestable customs that were practiced before you came and do not defile yourselves with them. I am the LORD your God."'
(Leviticus 18:1-4, 6, 16, 18-20, 22-28,30 NIV)

If we are sexually defiled we cannot honor God with our bodies. We become unholy. But without holiness, we cannot commune with God. Since our bodies are the temples of the Holy Spirit (the Spirit of God on earth), when we abuse, or contaminate it, we grieve the Holy Spirit, and cause Him to withdraw His help. Without the Holy Spirit, we are powerless against evil, and the devil. Purge yourself of all spiritual contaminants. Your body is not yours; it belongs to God. If you feel like having fun, follow your heart's dreams, but in the end, what matter most? Listen to the preacher:

Rejoice, O young man, in your adolescence, and let your heart cheer you in the days of your [full-grown] youth. And walk in the ways of your heart and in the sight of your eyes, but know that for all these things God will bring you into judgment. Therefore remove [the lusts that end in] sorrow and vexation from your heart and mind and put away evil from your body, for youth and the dawn of life are vanity [transitory, idle, empty, and devoid of truth]. (Ecclesiastes 11:9-10 AMP)

# Sexual Healing: Spiritual Detox

Put away the pornographic materials, and sever ties with the deceptive spirit that surrounds porno to interfere with your relationships. A gentleman seeking help from pornography wrote,

> I love my wife, but I've noticed that the more I use pornography, the less that I'm attracted to her physically. She's still pretty, but for some reason she just doesn't measure up anymore. How did that happen? *(Reaching out to* pornography *addicts and the people who love them. Answers to tough questions. Fires of Darkness Ministries. November 2004. )"*

As people become addicted to porn, over a period of time, their perception of beauty becomes distorted. As they covet and fantasize the body contours in women that they've seen portrayed in pornography, their acceptance of their wife's body changes. Slowly, their idea of normal sexual relations fades and becomes corrupted. As a result, they are not able to have a fulfilling sexual interaction with their spouse because they don't measure up. In the end the love for their spouse will fade, landing them in a vicious cycle of lust and covetousness that can never be fulfilled, as the demons of lust and fantasy play mind games with their sensuality. If you are a victim of pornography, you need to first disengage your mind. How?

Avoid watching or listening to x-rated materials. If you don't, the demons of perversion will entice you to act out your sexual hallucinations based on a one-sided fantasy relationship with someone instead of your mate. Of late, TV shows are pushing the envelope by televising sexual promiscuity and marriage-breaking materials to undermine the family structure, all in the name of adult entertainment. TV shows such as *Desperate Housewives,* glamorize moral decadence. They do nothing good for society and send the message that what we see happening around us is reality. But is what you experience, or see around you as reality, the truth?

How do we put a stop to this sexual craze from contaminating the sexual purity of our children? The answer lies in the realm of the spirit. It is not by accident that we see a correlation between parents who watch the show and its apparent popularity among children between nine to twelve years old. *(*http://www.cato.org/dailys/01-04-05.html Desperate Housewives *and Desperate Regulators-January 4, 2005)*.

Parental guidance, responsible government, and everybody playing his or her part are needed to put moderation in our adult inhibitions. Don't be surprised if these children grow up to see as harmless, and therefore mimic or act out, in their marriages what they saw portrayed on TV shows. Acting out may come in many ways. The push and pull of sexual sin is that "what goes in is what comes out." Don't feed your mind on sexual fantasies. Re-engage your mind and heart, and focus on purity and holiness. Since your spoken word is creative, be careful of what comes out of your mouth. It may defile you. Jesus told His disciples:

> But whatever comes out of the mouth comes from the heart, and this is what makes a man unclean and defiles [him]. For out of the heart come evil thoughts (reasonings and disputings and designs) such as murder, adultery, sexual vice, theft, false witnessing, slander, and irreverent speech.
>
> (Matthew 15:18-19)

> But immorality (sexual vice) and all impurity of lustful, rich, wasteful living] or greediness must not even be named among you, as is fitting and proper among saints (God's consecrated people).

> Let there be no filthiness (obscenity, indecency) nor foolish and sinful (silly and corrupt) talk, nor coarse jesting, which are not fitting or becoming; but instead voice your thankfulness [to God].

> For be sure of this: that no person practicing sexual vice or impurity in thought or in life, or one who is covetous [who

has lustful desire for the property of others and is greedy for gain]--for he [in effect] is an idolater--has any inheritance in the kingdom of Christ and of God.     (Ephesians 5:3-5 AMP)

Sinners are offered eternal life. But once we become Christians, we already have eternal life by the saving grace and sacrificial death of Christ on the cross. However, inheriting the kingdom of God depends on how well we run the race therefore, "I press on toward the goal to win the [supreme and heavenly] prize to which God in Christ Jesus is calling us upward" (Philippians 3:14 AMP). The writer of Hebrews has likened our lives to running in a race, so he says:

Wherefore seeing we also are compassed about with so great a cloud of witnesses, let us lay aside every weight, and the sin which doth so easily beset us, and let us run with patience the race that is set before us: Looking unto Jesus the author and finisher of our faith; who for the joy that was set before him endured the cross, despising the shame, and is set down at the right hand of the throne of God.          (Hebrews 12:1-2.)

Two things can hinder our spiritual progress, "sin" and "every weight". Sin disqualifies us from running for breaking the rules. However, running with unnecessary weights such as cares, burdens, and anxieties of life, or the love of this world will slow us down. But by faith in Jesus, we are to run "with patience," and perseverance, because the prize or reward is only given at the end of the race.

Don't be the conduit through which demons attack your family and marriage. Jesus warned the invalid He had healed at the pool of Bethesda to stop sinning, or something worse may happen to him (John 5:14). What is that "something" that could have happened to the man? In Matthew 12:43-45, Jesus warned us that when a demon is cast out it will get seven more demons, each stronger than the first, to try to get back in to further worsen the situation.

If you are worried about your sexual purity, and you have tried out everything but can't seem to get rid of the demons of sexual promiscuities, you need deliverance. This is a process by which demons of sexual perversion are cast out. Potentially, these spirits can ruin your sex life and marriage. They can also cause a lot of heartache for your family, the loss of your anointing, and the danger of not inheriting your reward from Jesus, although you are saved.

To rid yourself of sexual perversion and immorality on a permanent basis, you need to detoxify your body of any spiritual contaminants, and then observe the principles of biblical sexual practices. You also need to surrender yourself to Jesus Christ and make Him Lord and Master of your life. Ask Him to forgive your sins and cleanse your heart, mind, and soul of all sexual impurities. Any unconfessed sin in your life is grounds for spiritual attack, by the enemy as written:

> All that found them have devoured them: and their adversaries said, We offend not, because they have sinned against the LORD, the habitation of justice, even the LORD, the hope of their fathers. (Jeremiah 50:7)

Ask Jesus to come into your life based on His precious blood shed for you on the cross, so that you may be dead to sin and alive to God. Why the blood of Jesus, you may ask? It is divine truth that:

> Under the Law almost everything is purified by means of blood, and without the shedding of blood there is neither release from sin and its guilt nor the remission of the due and merited punishment for sins. (Hebrews 9:22 AMP)

It is through Jesus and the empowerment of the Holy Spirit can you receive and sustain healing, restoration of your sexual sanctity, and at the same time bring true joy to your life and marriage. In the Bible, we read that there is no salvation in any other but Jesus. Jesus, in John 14:6, says He is the "Way, Truth, and Life." Nobody can be united, with God, the Creator of heaven and earth, except through Him. If you feel there is something missing in your life, if you feel lonely and isolated, if you feel a void in your relationship, if you are craving for intimacy but looking in the wrong places, try Jesus. When you accept Jesus as your personal Savior, the Bible tells us in 2 Corinthians 5:17, you become a new creature; the old things (previous moral and spiritual conditions) are passed away, and all things become new. Your past and future sins are all forgiven.

Spiritually, you become like a virgin. He restores your spiritual purity. You become part of His divine church--His bride.

# Chapter Five

## Spiritual Marriage with a Curse

*When men began to increase in number on the earth and daughters were born to them, the sons of God saw that the daughters of men were beautiful, and they married any of them they chose.*

*(Genesis 6:1-2 NIV)*

*This too is a grievous evil: As a man comes, so he departs, and what does he gain, since he toils for the wind? All his days he eats in darkness, with great frustration, affliction and anger.*

*(Ecclesiastes 5:16-17 NIV)*

In this chapter, we shall explore, among other things, why and how evil spirits marry humans to overpower and sexually attack us, even in our dreams, to leave evil deposits that can adversely affect our lives.

During most deliverance ministrations that I have witnessed, spiritual marriages to demonic entities were more common among women. Satan knows that women are the primary agents for reproduction and for continuing the human species. So what better way to attack them, get a foothold in their lives to disrupt and destroy the family structure? Better still, why not marry them spiritually and forge a false alliance, using women as a weapon against humanity? In the Garden of Eden, when God cursed the serpent, He said:

> And I will put enmity between thee and the woman, and between thy seed and her seed; it shall bruise thy head, and thou shalt bruise his heel. (Genesis 3:15)

Don't get me wrong, I'm not saying women are evil incarnate. But because of their role and responsibility to populate the earth, they are often a magnet for demonic attacks to undermine their primary role as man's partner and helper.

According the Scriptures, sex unites two people spiritually as one. Sexual intercourse is therefore one of the primary weapons the devil uses against us. Engaging in casual or illicit sex can subject you to heavy spiritual bondage as demons are passed from one person to another. The physical manifestations of these spiritual bondages are the myriad psychological, emotional, medical, and marital problems that we assign to fate, luck, or poor interpersonal skills. When it comes to the spiritual, things you don't know can easily hurt and destroy you.

If your spiritual eyes were to be opened, to see the kind of spirits that inhabit or follow some people, you would understand why the Bible tells us to flee from all forms of sexual immoralities. People have said that when you sleep with somebody who has had multiple sexual partners, it is like sleeping with all those partners. That is precisely the truth. When you sleep with somebody, the two of you become one according to the Bible. Whatever evil spirits inhabited your sexual partner could also follow you as well.

## Ancestral Spiritual Marriages and Curses

There are gruesome spiritual marriage practices in the spiritual world. In my days as an usher in the Bronx, it was revealed to one lady during ministration that she was married to three evil spirits from three different countries. "How is this possible?" you may ask. Her family name was found in the three countries, and anyone with that name attracted a certain kind of spirit. In one country, it was the spirit of a dwarf; in another, a serpentine spirit; the third was a marine spirit. Over the years people have intermarried and moved from one country to another. Any association or covenant with a spiritual entity is valid anywhere you go until it is spiritually severed or annulled. For example, ancestral covenants or curses of one hundred, two hundred, three hundred, or more years remain enforceable, until they are broken or nullified spiritually.

Some years back, I spoke to an African-American woman who had visited the slave dungeons in Ghana to pray and break the curses that followed those who were sold into slavery in America. Look at the black-on-black crime and gang warfare in the United States. Some of this can be traced back to inter-tribal warfare in Africa, through the era of slavery during colonial America to present-day United States of America. These inter-tribal faction spirits of the ancestors still follow their descendants after all these years. Ancestral sins are often a source of hidden problems in our lives. Pray to break any generational sins and curses from falling on your children.

The Bible addresses the issue of generational curses. For example, Jacob cursed his firstborn son, Reuben, and the curse was so lethal it decimated the Reubenites for approximately 470 years (430 years in Egypt and 40 years in the wilderness). Not until Moses was about to die was the curse reversed. We read of this account in the Bible.

> While Israel was living in that region, Reuben went in and slept with his father's concubine Bilhah, and Israel heard of it.
>
> (Genesis 35:22 NIV)

In Egypt, when Jacob was about to die, he blessed and cursed some of his sons.

> Then Jacob called for his sons and said: "Gather around so I can tell you what will happen to you in days to come. Assemble and listen, sons of Jacob; listen to your father Israel. Reuben, you are my firstborn, my might, the first sign of my strength, excelling in honor, excelling in power. Turbulent as the waters,

> you will no longer excel, for you went up onto your father's bed,
> onto my couch and defiled it."          (Genesis 49:1-4 NIV)

The devastations we see among certain tribes by what we may label as misfortune are not necessarily coincidental. The descendants of Reuben lost their birthright due to the "sins of the fathers."

> The sons of Reuben the firstborn of Israel (he was the firstborn, but when he defiled his father's marriage bed, his rights as firstborn were given to the sons of Joseph son of Israel; so he could not be listed in the genealogical record in accordance with his birthright.          (1 Chronicles 5:1 NIV)

Moses witnessed firsthand the decimating effect of the curse on the Reubenites, and so before he died, he prayed to reverse the curse by declaring, "Let Reuben live and not die, nor his men be few" (Deuteronomy 33:6 NIV).

Some parents place a curse on their children when they call them by derogatory names. Jacob cursed his own children and the results were devastating. When you are angry, be careful of your choice of words. You may be helping Satan plant curses on your own family and descendants. Be careful, our spoken words are creative.

## Be Careful of Your "Sweet Nothings"

At one time during ministration, my pastor asked a lady, "Who is John?" The lady thought for a moment, then laughed. She said when she was a child, her mother jokingly asked her, "Among all these children (her playmates) who do you love?" She said, "John." Immediately, whatever spirit was following John started following her.

To this day, this lady has not been able to marry. No one who comes into her life is "good enough." She thinks she is the one making the decision. No! The spirit drives away potential soul mates. After all, out of her own mouth she confessed that she loved John. There is death and life in the power of the tongue, so be careful of the words that come out of your mouth. Don't smooth-talk your way to fulfill

97

your sexual desires; you could be your own worst enemy.

> He who guards his lips guards his life, but he who speaks
> rashly will come to ruin. A fool's mouth is his undoing, and
> his lips are a snare to his soul.　　(Proverbs 13:3; 18:7 NIV.)

## My Funny Valentine with a Curse

A visiting pastor to our church recalled a deliverance session in which a woman being delivered spoke out in a male voice. The voice was that of a demon, a local river god, who refused to be cast out, protesting that the couple had come to him for help. Apparently, this woman and her fiancé had gone to a fetish shrine to seal their love for each other, and to exclude all others from their union. At the shrine, they entered into a blood covenant. Blood was drawn from their fingertips, put into a bowl, and mixed with some potion. They were then made to drink the concoction. After a while, this woman came across a man who had returned home to Ghana from Germany. This "bogga" guy seduced the woman, and she fell in love with him. (Those returning home from Hamburg, or Germany are fondly called "bogga," like the Yanki or Yankees from the USA.)

Sometime later, this woman experienced a deadly rash on her body called ananse. She decided to seek help and ended up at the deliverance session. Eventually, the river god was cast out, and the woman received her deliverance. She was also healed of the deadly rash. Don't interfere in other people's marriages. You may attract a curse. In fact, one lady recently died in London when a death spell was cast on her for going after someone's husband. She died of leukemia.

## Evil Spiritual Ruler

I have wondered why the early Christian churches practiced spiritual warfare and the casting out of demons, yet today some in the churches frown upon it with uneasiness. No wonder there are too many spiritually impotent people in the churches, who have no clue as to what is happening around them. In Ecclesiastes we read:

> There is an evil I have seen under the sun, the sort or error
> that arises from a ruler; I have seen slaves on horseback, while
> princes go on foot like slaves.        (Ecclesiastes 10:5, 7)

As Christians, we should rule over the spirits who have come to "steal, kill, and destroy" us.

During one ministration that I witnessed, a demon being cast out protested, saying, "I have been ruling this family for seven hundred years, and you think you are going to cast me out?"

An evil spirit ruler over your family or clan can deny you what God gave you from birth, saying that you belong to him because of a covenant some ancestor entered on your behalf, even before your parents were born, or because of some spiritual debt and therefore whatever you have, including your children, belongs to him. Even upon your death, spiritual creditors can still harass your seed.

> The wife of a man from the company of the prophets cried out
> to Elisha, "Your servant my husband is dead, and you know
> that he revered the LORD. But now his creditor is coming to
> take my two boys as his slaves"        (2 Kings 4:1 NIV).

Many men have financial problems, always short on cash and living from hand to mouth. If you are experiencing financial problems, or you are riddled with debt, you may be experiencing a situation where your money is being frittered away for other uses in the realm of the spirit.

Gross mismanagement of your finances including compulsive gambling can be spiritually induced. There may also be a spiritual embargo on your finances, which could result in job and business losses. Even a partial embargo would manifest in trickle-down gains or profits, not enough to sustain any meaningful growth.

In the end, financial insecurity can lead to frustration, emotional and psychological problems to adversely affect your marriage and further undermine the family structure. It is not uncommon to find rich and affluent people commit suicide. Money cannot solve your problems, or buy you peace, if the evil ruler over your family decides to deny you the enjoyment of your wealth. It is written:

> And this, too, is a very serious problem. As people come into this world, so they depart. All their hard work is for nothing. They have been working for the wind, and everything will be swept away. Throughout their lives, they live under a cloud-- frustrated, discouraged, and angry.
> (Ecclesiastes 10:5, 7; 5:16-17 NLT)

Find out from your family history, which ancestral spirits rule over your clan or family. You need to break off any generational curses you have inherited as a result of the activities of evil spiritual rulers.

When you pray, stand on the Word of God, and tell the demons to relinquish their hold on the divine plan of our Creator for us to eat, drink, and find satisfaction in our labor during the few days of life He has given us. Your blessing from God is to work, and to enjoy your wealth and possessions. However, when we violate God's spiritual laws, we forfeit our rights. The preacher in Ecclesiastes says:

> I have seen another evil under the sun, and it weighs heavily on men: God gives a man wealth, possessions and honor, so that he lacks nothing his heart desires, but God does not enable him to enjoy them, and a stranger enjoys them instead. This is meaningless and a grievous evil.        (Ecclesiastes 6:1-2)

When you come under spiritual attack from the devil, the key is to stand on the Word of God:

> In those days, people will live in the houses they build and eat the fruit of their own vineyards.
> It will not be like the past, when invaders took the houses and confiscated the vineyards. For my people will live as long as trees and will have time to enjoy their hard-won gains.
> They will not work in vain, and their children will not be doomed to misfortune. For they are people blessed by the LORD, and their children, too, will be blessed.
> I will answer them before they even call to me. While they are still talking to me about their needs, I will go ahead and answer their prayers!        (Isaiah 65:21-24 NLT)

Stand on the above verses and demand your right to enjoy your family, and your God-given gifts in peace if you are not living unrighteously. The least, but the most important thing you can do is to pray, and cry to God for help.

I cannot overemphasize the importance of spiritual warfare prayers; besides, the Bible tells us to pray without ceasing with all manner of prayers. This is a directive from God. It is for your own protection.

## A Man's Enemies Are within His Own Family

Your gift from God is to be able to enjoy all the good things He has given you without any interference from the devil. However, the sad part of this interference is that the agents of these demonic spiritual attacks are often members of one's own family, through the activities of household witchcraft. But the Bible in Proverbs 11:29 warns, "He that troubleth his own house shall inherit the wind." When it comes to witchcraft, no spiritual enemy can get to you without the help of an inside job. Your own household may betray and sell you out. Here is some advice from the Bible:

> Trust ye not in a friend, put ye not confidence in a guide: keep the doors of thy mouth from her that lieth in thy bosom. For the son dishonoureth the father, the daughter riseth up against her mother, the daughter in law against her mother in law; a man's enemies are the men of his own house.   (Micah 7:5-6)

During a ministration in the Bronx, New York, the pastor revealed to a woman who was having marital problems that at the time of her engagement, the household witches from her side of the family, and the husband's side had a spiritual meeting, and decided that the marriage would last twenty seven years, and after that it should break. In a situation like this, no amount of human counseling can save the marriage. Those who know spiritual matters, and have been instructed in the art of spiritual warfare, can break the yoke placed on such a marriage, through fasting and prayers.

Witchcraft is one of the dominant methods Satan uses to decimate and devastate families. Even a perceived threat or sheer envy can get you into trouble. You can be summoned to a court spiritually, and in most cases you will be found guilty. You will be sentenced, and woe to you if you're not a child of God, or are a child who is not living righteously or knows nothing about spiritual warfare. Always stand on the word of God and claim your deliverance. Declare and decree:

> [Therefore] I will look unto the LORD; I will wait for the God
> of my salvation: my God will hear me. Rejoice not against me,
> O mine enemy: when I fall, I shall arise; when I sit in darkness,
> the LORD shall be a light unto me.           (Micah 7:7-8)

## The Mother-in-Law vs. Daughter-in-Law Syndrome

According to the Bible, the spiritual head of a woman in a marriage is her man, the desire of her heart. But demonic spirits would have none of that, and so any determination to make the marriage work will be met by strong resistance, either from the woman's or the man's side of the family, to break up the marriage.

In the realm of the spirit in the demonic world, the lines between marriages can be blurred. For example, in witchcraft, a sister can be married to her own brother or other male members in the family for the purpose of controlling their marriage. Although demonic spirits like to marry women in the family, men are not immune from this unholy matrimony. In some instances, a man can be turned into what is called "household gentleman" or "family elder." He becomes preoccupied with the affairs of the family. Such a man does not listen to his wife, but only to his side of the family, especially his mother.

In the West, these men are labeled as "mama's boys." Any overt dictates of a matriarch over the marital affairs of her son should be frowned upon with suspicion. If a mother's "love" is smothering the marriage, the couple needs prayers. The matriarch may have been married to her own son spiritually. So when a young wife cannot stand her mother-in-law, the root cause may be spiritual. The spiritual desire to control the man pits the mother-in-law against the daughter in-law. However, there can only be one queen in the family.

Sometimes, a man can be turned into a womanizer or a spiritual prostitute. He may have been betrothed to a spiritual entity in childhood, so growing up he is not able to date one girl at a time. As an adult, even if he gets married, he cannot live with one woman for long, and in most cases, joy in marriage is out of the question. If you are a Christian, stand on the Word of God. Open your mouth and declare your right to enjoy your marriage. God has already decreed:

> Therefore shall a man leave his father and his mother, and shall cleave unto his wife: and they shall be one flesh.
> (Genesis 2:24)

> Enjoy life with the woman whom you love all the days of your fleeting life which He has given to you under the sun; for this is your reward in life and in your toil in which you have labored under the sun. (Ecclesiastes 9:9 NASB)

Ladies, if you are experiencing troubles in your marriage, open your eyes and be alert to demonic influences that may be impacting your relationship. Your men could be under tremendous spiritual attacks, even from their own families. Never stop praying for your family, and especially for your marriage. When you pray, reject every evil spiritual suitor, husband, wife, child, engagement, marriage, gift, money, friend, or relative dogging your life, and command them in the name of Jesus to leave you and never come back.

## Delayed or Denied Marriages

Household witchcraft can spiritually turn a woman into a man, in which case the woman cannot conceive and have children. This woman could be a professional woman, very rich and attractive, but unable to have a husband or children. This is to make sure that her wealth is used to look after her extended family. She may have men in her life and cohabitate, but not marriage.

Some time ago, a lady shared a testimony with the congregation at our church in the Bronx, in which she said that in her family, most of the women have children from different fathers because their partners don't stay in the relationship. Spiritually, the men are driven away from the women. A woman could work and make money but that is all. Any time she is engaged to a man, the relationship is put on life support, and the engagement does not blossom into a marriage. If a marriage was consummated, and a wedding took place, the man died. Black widowhood is not a myth. It is a spiritual phenomenon, and physical reality.

She said the men in her family were all handsome, and talented but were always broke and couldn't sustain a marriage. They became womanizers, and if they fathered children, they were incapable of caring for them.

The woman who shared the above testimony was the same lady who, during her deliverance, had a demon spoke through her, saying, "I have been ruling this family for 700 years, and you think you are going to cast me out?" If you are experiencing lateness getting married, put your trust and hope in the Lord. The Bible assures us that delayed is not denied:

> For the vision is yet for an appointed time and it hastens to the end [fulfillment]; it will not deceive or disappoint. Though it tarry, wait [earnestly] for it, because it will surely come; it will not be behindhand on its appointed day.
>
> (Habakkuk 2:3 AMP)

> Seek out of the book of the Lord and read: not one of these [details of prophecy] shall fail, none shall want and lack her mate [in fulfillment]. For the mouth [of the Lord] has comman-ded, and His Spirit has gathered them.
>
> (Isaiah 34:16 AMP)

God has made everything beautiful in its time (Ecclesiastes 3:11). People should examine themselves concerning the divine purpose of holy matrimony. They should seek spiritual premarital counseling or the biblical advice of those who have been able to stay married through thick and thin, "for richer or poorer," and "in sickness and in health." Have you ever heard of the "seven-year itch" in marriage? During this time, any little disagreement gets blown out of proportion. Demons can interfere with the communication and thought processes of people to ruin relationships. When this happens, no amount of relationship-building skills can save the marriage, if the source of the problem is not recognized as spiritual, and dealt with accordingly.

The spiritual realm is powerful, superimposed, and intertwined with the physical. Therefore people should try to understand the spiritual rules and guidelines concerning human sexuality and purity, even before they start dating, certainly before they start having sex, and definitely before tying the nuptial cord. Ignorance or complacency in these areas will not indemnify anyone of the ramifications associated with violations of laws concerning to our sexuality, sex, and marriage, whether they are Christians or not. Couples should not be pressured into marriage, because life is war, and marriage is one of the battlegrounds, to fight against all intruders to the union.

## Dreams as Sources of Spiritual Bondage

According to *Merriam-Webster Collegiate Dictionary*:

> **Incubus** is an evil spirit that lies on persons in their sleep; especially one that has sexual intercourse with women while they are sleeping.

> **Succubus** is a demon assuming female form to have sexual intercourse with men in their sleep.

Have you ever had any sexual encounters in your dreams? I have. When I didn't know any better, I thought it was normal. But when I found out the real spiritual implication, I was angry, I felt violated. Those who lack spiritual knowledge believe that all dreams are imaginations of our subconsciousness. But remember this, any form of sexual encounters in your dreams may be demonic. Why? If any sexual intercourse, other than with your spouse, is prohibited in the physical so it is in the realm of the spirit. So be careful of any nocturnal visitors, or Incubus and Succubus spirits who come to romance or sleep with you in your dreams. Be careful of wet dreams, or nocturnal emissions. Definitely avoid masturbation (solo sex), which opens you to demonic infestation. It is written, "For ye are bought with a price: therefore glorify God in your body, and in your spirit, which are God's" (1 Corinthians 6:20).

When faced with spiritual sexual assaults, prayerfully cancel and neutralize any evil deposits that may later become a source of trouble in your life. When you pray, bind and paralyze any strongman assigned to curse and lock your womb or reproductive organs. In the name of Jesus, rebuke the spirits and command them to leave and never come to you again. Then commit your sexual life to Jesus.

If you are leading a life of sexual promiscuity, put an end to it. Avoid becoming a casualty. Don't let your marriage be part of the divorce statistics. Repent, and ask the Lord for forgiveness and for the Holy Spirit to empower you to put an end to your sexual immoralities. If you don't, the demons will come back, and the battle for your freedom will be seven times, harder.

## Evil Deposits

There are many ways evil spirits try to attack us. One of them is through our dreams. God puts a hedge around people, and demons attack them when this hedge is broken and a point of contact is achieved (Ecclesiastes 10:8). When the hedge is broken, demons have the right to attack you. However, the demons cannot overcome you until a spiritual seed is sown in your life.

Through sexual intercourse in your dreams, an evil deposit can be become a curse in your life. A curse sown in your womb will fight against your pregnancy and cause other infertility problems, including ovarian cancer. The curse must be broken before anyone can be set free from this pattern of evil. We serve a living God, an omnipotent God, whose Word is Spirit and life. Have faith; God's Word is already settled in heaven, therefore He watches to perform it.

## The Word of God is Fire

Is not my word like as a fire? saith the LORD; and like a hammer that breaketh the rock in pieces?          (Jeremiah 23:29)

Wherefore thus saith the LORD God of hosts, Because ye speak this word, behold, I will make my words in thy mouth fire, and this people wood, and it shall devour them.          (Jeremiah 5:14)

The Word of God on your lips will function like fire and hammer to break, consume, and dissolve every fibroid, cancer, ovarian cyst, or other demonic deposit in your body. By faith, open your mouth, decree, and declare the Word because the Bible assures us saying:

Thou shalt also decree a thing, and it shall be established unto thee: and the light shall shine upon thy ways.          (Job 22:28)

Stand on the Scriptures; claim your healing by faith in the name of Jesus. For your deliverance, put your hand on where you have been afflicted. Call on the name of God, Jehovah Nissi (your Conqueror and Banner), and command any demons assigned to your situation to break loose and go. Ask them to take away their evil deposits and leave you in peace. Call on the name of God, Jehovah Rapheka (your Healer) to restore your health. There is healing, and deliverance power in the Word of God. Let us, therefore, be in one accord in saying:

Bless the LORD, O my soul: and all that is within me, bless his holy name. Bless the LORD, O my soul, and forget not all his benefits: Who forgiveth all thine iniquities; who healeth all thy diseases; Who redeemeth thy life from destruction; who crowneth thee with lovingkindness and tender mercies.
(Psalm 103:1-4)

# Barrenness

Barrenness does not mean that your world has come to an end. God shut the wombs of both Rachel and Hannah. Perhaps He did this so His glory could be displayed in the lives of these women. Hear what Jesus said about a man who was born blind from birth.

> AS HE passed along, He noticed a man blind from his birth. His disciples asked Him, Rabbi, who sinned, this man or his parents, that he should be born blind? Jesus answered, It was not that this man or his parents sinned, but he was born blind in order that the workings of God should be manifested (displayed and illustrated) in him.                    (John 9:1-3 AMP)

Rachel later gave birth to Joseph and Benjamin, who bear the names of two of the twelve ancestral tribes of the Israelites. Hannah gave birth to Samuel, one of the greatest prophets in the Bible. Just as God shut down the wombs of these women, Satan and his agents can shut down the wombs of their victims.

Some people cannot have children for a variety of reasons because of what the devil and his agents have done to them. Evil spirits can put a spiritual covering over the womb of women, or have their ovaries removed, or place an evil deposit in the womb to fight against any pregnancies. Be on your guard; birth defects and other infertility problems can be spiritually induced. If you need help, stand firmly on the following verses and pray for your deliverance.

> And if you hearken to these precepts and keep and do them, the Lord your God will keep with you the covenant and the steadfast love which He swore to your fathers. And He will love you, bless you, and multiply you; He will also bless the fruit of your body and the fruit of your land, your grain, your new wine, and your oil, the increase of your cattle and the young of your flock in the land, which He swore to your fathers to give you. You shall be blessed above all peoples; there shall not be male or female barren among you, or among your cattle. And the Lord will take away from you all sickness, and none of the evil diseases of Egypt which you knew will He put upon you, but will lay them upon all who hate you.
> (Deuteronomy 7:12-15)

Just as people renounce marriage to lead a celibate life for Kingdom reasons, the devil and his agents can prevent people from gainful marriages. How? Just look around you, and see how people choose to live their lives. We see all kinds of alternative family structures and relationships such as cohabitation, open marriages, polygamy, gay and lesbian marriages, and those who consider themselves transgendered. This may amaze you, but there are women in this world whose hands have never been asked in marriage, and those who have been refused or accepted into marriage. This too is the work of the enemy. These women are spiritually seen either as male or something else other than female! The good news is that, for all the feminine aching hearts who have longed to be married and have children, being childless or never being married, does not mean that your world has come to an end if you are a Christian. There are two beautiful passages in Isaiah that seem to suggest that childlessness on earth could indicate more superior (spiritual) children. It is written:

> SING, O barren one, you who did not bear; break forth into singing and cry aloud, you who did not travail with child! For the [spiritual] children of the desolate one will be more than the children of the married wife, says the Lord. For your Maker is your Husband--the Lord of hosts is His name--and the Holy One of Israel is your Redeemer; the God of the whole earth He is called. (Isaiah 54:1, 5 AMP)

This is a spiritual mystery. Let's search the Scripture for some answers. According to Jesus, unless a man is born again spiritually, he cannot enter into the kingdom of God.

> Jesus answered, I assure you, most solemnly I tell you, unless a man is born of water and [even] the Spirit, he cannot [ever] enter the kingdom of God. What is born of [from] the flesh is flesh [of the physical is physical]; and what is born of the Spirit is spirit. (John 3:5-6 AMP)

Anytime God saves someone, that person receives a new resurrected soul; he is born again. After that, spiritual mentorship becomes very important, this transcends biological lines. For example, when we look at the relationship between Paul and Timothy, we find that Paul was a mentor to Timothy. Paul therefore imparted godly wisdom and teachings to Timothy, for him to be able to teach, nurture, and raise God's children on biblical truths and principles. He reminded Timothy as follows:

> You, however, know all about my teaching, my way of life, my purpose, faith, patience, love, endurance; But as for you, continue in what you have learned and have become convinced of, because you know those from whom you learned it, and how from infancy you have known the holy Scriptures, which are able to make you wise for salvation through faith in Christ Jesus. (2 Timothy 3:10, 14-15 NIV)

> And the things you have heard me say in the presence of many witnesses entrust to reliable men who will also be qualified to teach others. (2 Timothy 2:2 NIV)

Whoever God uses to bring His plan to fruition is a spiritual parent to that individual. People are birthed into the kingdom of God when the saints intercede for them to receive the Gospel. God does the actual saving but we labor with Him in His vineyard. Those who support the work of the Lord for people to be born again share an inheritance with Jesus Christ in His kingdom.

Those who have been unable to bear their own children can have the assurance that the Lord can use them to birth, or nurture children into His kingdom when they give of their talent, time, and treasure to win souls. This is a far greater reward than physical birth. According to Proverbs 11:30, "Those who win souls are wise." Taking a child under your tutelage to teach spiritual principles and truths from the Bible can provide a strong father figure they lack, or never had.

## Satan's Evil Counterfeits

Just as God changed Abraham's name from Abram ("exalted father") to Abraham ("father of many"), and Jacob's name from Jacob ("he grasps the heel; figuratively, he deceives") to Israel (he struggles with God [and with men and have overcome]), Satan can spiritually change your name to a name that attracts hardship.

In some societies, the names parents give to their children denote hardship or even death. Sometimes they are named after or dedicated to a river god or some powerful demon. The rationale in these cases is usually to attract the "blessings" of the spirits.

In the Bible, we also find names such as Jabez, which means, "sorrow." When Jabez realized the negative impact his name was having on his life, he asked God for help. The account is recorded in 1 Chronicles.

> Jabez was more honorable than his brothers. His mother had named him Jabez, saying, "I gave birth to him in pain." Jabez cried out to the God of Israel, "Oh, that you would bless me and enlarge my territory! Let your hand be with me, and keep me from harm so that I will be free from pain." And God granted his request. (1 Chronicles 4:9-10 NIV)

Here is a fascinating and powerful spiritual insight. Names are very important, so be careful what you name your child. By name you call and get the attention of some entities. A child named after an evil person will attract evil spirits. If a spirit of divorce or barrenness inhabited or followed the person after whom you named your child, that child may end up barren or go through divorce as well. The expression "He is a chip off the old block" is a physical as well as a spiritual reality. If the meaning of your name denotes hardship, you may consider changing it, or asking God to change your name to one that will bring you blessings. Pray that any problems attached to your name or family name will be neutralized in the name of Jesus.

## Demonic Marks and Signs

Jesus promised the abundant life, so if you are walking uprightly, why haven't you been able to enjoy your blessings and material prosperity here on earth? There may be a hidden curse operating in your life. Just as God put a mark on Cain so that anyone who found him would not kill him (Genesis 4:15), evil spirits are able to put a mark on somebody for destruction, or hardship such as financial hardships, separation, disappointment, setback, failed health, and even death. You, or your marriage can easily be marked "For Sale" and sold spiritually without your knowledge. When this happens, in the realm of the spirit, your wedding ring could be missing from your finger, or replaced with cursed demonic rings. This could result in marital anomalies, which can lead to failed relationships, and even divorce. God wants you to fully enjoy all the good things He has given you in peace, without any demonic interference.

Pray and ask Jesus to cleanse you of all demonic marks and signs with His atoning blood. Plead His blood to nullify all curses operating in your life.

## Beware of Gifts, Jewelry, and Flea Market Bargains

During a deliverance session in the Bronx, the pastor called a young black girl to the front. When questioned about a choker necklace, she said a white lady had given it to her as a gift. Unknown to this lady, the choker was actually a spiritual device to monitor her every move. The pastor told her that the donor of the gift had "bought" her spiritually (perhaps sold by her own people) and that the gift served as a point of contact. He also revealed to her that, every Tuesday, the donor of the gift went under the sea, and sometimes spent seven days in the heart of the earth. Eventually, the young girl would have been married spiritually to the gift donor. She would not be able to marry or sustain a viable marriage. She could even have ended up barren.

Ladies, when you receive a gift from anybody, pray and plead the blood of Jesus over it before using it. When you buy anything from a store, pray over it. People have bought jewelry from reputable stores that turned out to be satanic goods and served as a point of contact to harass their lives. Usually when our pastor sees any demonic item, the first question is, "Where did you get this?" Most of the time, it was bought from a flea market. But once a while, it is from a regular store. Be careful of flea markets bargains and garage sales, they could be discarded items of accursed inheritance.

When you receive a gift, open it right away to avoid having accursed items in your house to unleash curses on your family. People have received wedding gifts that were demonic items to cause the breakup of their marriage. Not all who show up for a wedding or marriage are in favor of the couple being together. Beware! Through the gifts, the seed for the destruction of the marriage may have been sown, even when the marriage vows, were being exchanged.

## Evil behind the Mask

Demons have been known to attack their victims by using the faces of other people. During one ministration in the Bronx, demons used the face of a wife to torment her husband. The plan was to get the husband to believe that his wife was a witch. This could have led to the breakup of the marriage. The devil always wants to set people up for trouble. Seek wisdom and spiritual discernment.

Pray against all chameleon demons that Satan has assigned to use your face to bewitch and afflict people in their dreams. Ask that all enemies in disguise be forced by God to reveal their identities. Rebuke and bind all the demons that give people evil dreams concerning you, to imagine evil about you, to gossip and tell lies about you, in order to create confusion, tension, and hatred between you and your spouse, family members, and other people. Pray and command that no witch or wizard use your face or name to attack anybody in his or her dream. The same goes for dream attackers who may use your face to violate other people by romancing and having sex with them in their dreams. Don't limit your understanding to only scientific, or physiological explanations for dreams. Don't listen, or misled by those who believe dreams have no adaptive purposes. Listen to Job, as he recollects an encounter he had in his dreams:

> A word came to me in secret-- a mere whisper of a word, but I heard it clearly. It came in a scary dream one night, after I had fallen into a deep, deep sleep. Dread stared me in the face, and Terror. I was scared to death--I shook from head to foot.
> (Job 4:12-14 MSG)

## Spiritual Mind and Soul Ties

> And it came to pass, when he had made an end of speaking
> unto Saul, that the soul of Jonathan was knit with the soul of
> David, and Jonathan loved him as his own soul.
>
> (1 Samuel 18:1)

David loved Jonathan like his brother. However, the souls of men
and women can also knit together with negative repercussions. As
mentioned earlier, sexual partners can pass on a multitude of evil
spirits through sex, thereby subjecting their victims to heavy spiritual
bondage. This could also lead to the knitting of souls together. Often
the souls of ex-lovers knit together, even though they no longer see
each other. I'm not saying or suggesting that David and Jonathan
were sexual partners. The word *love* in the above Bible verse is
anything but erotic love.

Be very careful of your folklore heroes (i.e. celebrities, superstars,
gurus, and the people you adore). Don't utter anything rash from
your mouth, and thus get ensnared by whatever spiritual entities that
either inhabited or followed these people. These spirits are always
looking for an invitation to indwell people. Don't become your own
worst enemy.

Don't overly cling to items belonging to loved ones who have
passed on; you may be unwittingly calling up whatever spirits were
associated with the dead person. A visit to a cemetery or graveside
of a loved one should be a time of remembrance, not a search for help.
You may not know it, but you could be engaging in necromancy. In
the Bible, God warns us against ancestral worship.

> And when the people [instead of putting their trust in God] shall
> say to you, Consult for direction mediums and wizards who
> chirp and mutter, should not a people seek and consult their
> God? Should they consult the dead on behalf of the living?
>
> (Isaiah 8:19)

To those who are spiritually impotent or dead, there is hope in Jesus.
In John 5:25 He says, "Verily, verily, I say unto you, the hour is
coming, and now is, when the dead shall hear the voice of the Son

of God: and they that hear shall live." Seek to hear the voice of Jesus and you shall receive power, because His words are spirit and life. Amen.

## God's Power is Available to You

According to the Bible, there will come a time when the saints (the true believers, the followers of Jesus Christ) will judge angels. But even here on earth, tremendous power is still available to us through our Lord Jesus. From the Bible we are assured that:

> The Father loves the Son and has placed everything in his hands.　　　　　　　　　　　　　　　　　(John 3:35 NIV)

> Then Jesus came to them and said, "All authority in heaven and on earth has been given to me."　　(Matthew 28:18 NIV)

Again, the Bible tells us in 1 Corinthians 4:20, that the kingdom of God is about power and empowered life and not a matter of talk. We need God's mighty weapons, not mere worldly weapons, to fight our spirituals battles to knock down the devil's strongholds. First of all, what can we do, to avail ourselves of these weapons? Second, how do we free ourselves from all illicit spiritual marriage, or demonic bondage? The solution is simple if you are a child of God and a born-again believer. In the name of Jesus take authority over these intruders, use the Scriptures by faith, and stand on the Word of God to deal with your particular situation. For example, to sever, or annul any evil spiritual marriage, in your prayers, you could pray as follows:

> *Listen to me, you evil spirit, or whatever you are, and married to me spiritually. I stand in the anointing of the Holy Spirit, and declare and decree the Word of God, His mandate for humans to be married to humans and not to evil spirits, and also for a woman to have sex with a man, not with demonic spirits. Any unlawful sexual intercourse with humans, whether spiritually or physically, is a violation of God's law.*

*In the name of Jesus, and by the power of the Holy Spirit, I divorce myself and sever all ties to any demonic spiritual marriages. My Lord Jesus Christ, and the Holy Spirit are my advocates; and therefore I cannot lose. I command every satanic ring, and wedding dress to burn in the name of Jesus. I cancel, I renounce, and I erase every point of contact by which these spiritual marriages were arranged and consummated.*

*I command all demonic forces manipulating, delaying or hindering my earthly marriage to be completely paralyzed, in the victorious name of Jesus. The Bible says, "Whoever the Son shall set free, is free indeed" John 8:36. I have been set free by the saving power of the blood of Jesus. I am a winner. I am an overcomer.*

*From today onward, I receive an injunction against you from my Father, the great Judge in heaven. If you attempt to sleep with me again, may the fire of the Holy Spirit torment and consume you, in the mighty name of Jesus Christ, I command. Amen!*

Anyone who has had any sexual encounters in his, or her dreams ought to seriously consider the issues raised in the above prayers, to break any yokes, curses, and any evil deposits. Jesus has given you power and authority. Use it.

As long as this world is in place, there will always be continual struggle between the good and evil, the wicked and the righteous, the holy and the unholy. The apostle Paul reminds us of our fight against spiritual wickedness in high places. If you ignore Paul's warning, or take lightly what Jesus said concerning the devil, evil spirits have a field day, devastating and decimating your family with all kinds of afflictions and calamities.

If you need assurance from the Word of God, here are some powerful Scripture verses for use against satanic yokes, demonic infestations, including all addictions. Open your mouth and pray:

> Then the LORD put forth his hand and touch my mouth. And the LORD said to me, behold, I have put my words in thy mouth. See, I have this day set thee over the nations and over the kingdoms, to root out and to pull down, and to destroy, and throw down, and to build, and to plant. (Jeremiah 1:9-10)

> Wherefore thus saith the LORD God of hosts, because ye speak this word, behold, I will make my words in thy mouth fire, and this people wood, and it shall devour them. (Jeremiah 5: 14)

> I tell you the truth, whatever you bind on earth will be bound in heaven, and whatever you loose on earth will be loosed in heaven. (Matthew 18:18 NIV)

> Truly I tell you, whoever says to this mountain, Be lifted up and thrown into the sea! And does not doubt at all in his heart but believes that what he says will take place, it will be done for him. For this reason I am telling you, whatever you ask for in prayer, believe (trust and be confident) that it is granted to you, and you will [get it]. (Mark 11:23-24 AMP)

> So now, I will break his yoke bar from upon you, and I will tear off your shackles. (Nahum 1:13 NASB)

> In that day, declares the LORD Almighty, I will break the yoke off their necks and will tear off their bonds; no longer will foreigners enslave them. (Jeremiah 30:8 NIV)

> And it shall come to pass in that day, that his burden shall be taken away from off your neck, and the yoke shall be destroyed because of the anointing. (Isaiah 10:27)

> [*Heavenly Father, I thank you*]: For thou hast broken the yoke of his burden, and the staff of his shoulder, the rod of his oppressor, as in the day of Midian. {*Comments added*} (Isaiah 9:4)

If you have been having nightmares or insomnia, before you go to bed, you may incorporate the following, as part of your prayers:

*Heavenly Father, in the name of Jesus Christ of Nazareth, my Savior, Redeemer, Liberator, and Protector, I commit myself, and my property to Your care. I cover myself with the blood of Jesus. I take authority over all nocturnal visitors; demons of sex, demons of nightmares, and all evil spirits assigned to attack me through dreams. I bind them in seven ways; I render their plans and works null and void. I cripple their powers, and in the name of Jesus I cast them out of my dreams. I renounce, revoke and repudiate any allegiance, or covenants that I made, or were enacted on my behalf. I break every demonic yoke that has been put on me.*

*Heavenly Father, please release Your mighty warrior angels to protect me, my property and everything that belongs to me or has been entrusted to my care. I will have a peaceful sleep, and I will be refreshed, and strengthened in the morning to declare the glory of the Lord. In the mighty name of Jesus I pray. Amen!*

# Chapter Six

## Marital Anomalies and Counseling

*Preach the word; be instant in season, out of season; reprove, rebuke, exhort with all long suffering and doctrine. For the time will come when they will not endure sound doctrine; but after their own lusts shall they heap to themselves teachers, having itching ears; And they shall turn away their ears from the truth, and shall be turned unto fables.* (2 Timothy 4:2-4 NIV)

*Be not deceived; God is not mocked: for whatsoever a man soweth, that shall he also reap. For he that soweth to his flesh shall of the flesh reap corruption; but he that soweth to the Spirit shall of the Spirit reap life everlasting.* (Galatians 6:7-8)

Much has been written on marriage counseling based on psychoanalytic and behavioral deductions. Good communication and interpersonal skills are important but the influence of the spiritual is much more powerful. People spend a lot time and resources in material preparation when getting married. But one area often overlooked, is the spiritual teachings and guidelines needed to maintain and sustain the marriage.

# The Garden Called Marriage

Your marriage is like a garden. The responsibilities of both partners should mirror the charge God gave Adam and Eve to take care of the Garden of Eden. In gardening, there are three fundamental considerations that can provide the basis for good seed germination and subsequent growth of crops. These are :(1) deep soil, (2) well-drained soil, and (3) soil high in organic content.

First, the couple should be prepared to plow the marriage soil by committing to a deeper understanding of the ideals of the marriage union, based on abilities with regard to their talents, time, and treasure. The marriage union is as much a spiritual union as well as physical. Therefore whenever one aspect of it, especially the spiritual is neglected or missing, the marriage is susceptible to endure poor growth, fall apart and end in divorce. In order to resurrect the marriage, you need to examine yourselves and find answers to some of the following questions.

What is marriage? Who designed the marriage institution and why? Why should I marry? Whom do I want to marry and why? How would my in-laws, friends, colleagues, and others likely impact our marriage for good or bad? How can we safely navigate through the physical and spiritual storms of holy matrimony? Who can we rely on to help us with our marriage when overwhelmed with marital problems?

Marriage is hard work, but in the end you will enjoy the fruits of your labor. But be careful of those who would attempt to steal or destroy the fruits of your marriage.

The second consideration for lasting growth is a well-drained marital soil, or an environment where the couple lets go of all unscriptural notions of a marriage union. The first question you may ask yourself is whose voice do you hear in your marriage? Any counsel that seeks to cause confusion and rift in your marriage cannot be the counsel of God. God is not the author of confusion. If you love your mate, and want your relationship to grow and evolve, you have to discard all the excess baggage of hurts and pains of past relationships. Her problem should be your problem. The Problem should be labeled "our" problem so both of you can work at it. As long as it is her problem or his problem, you may not help in finding a lasting solution. The husband and wife must trust each other and work collectively as a team to maintain and sustain the home.

Another question you may ask yourself is "who are you at home?" Don't let your position outside the home ruin your marriage. Most of the current literature on relationships encourages individuals to look out for themselves, each to their own best interest, with one open eye as to what the other person is doing. No wonder, nowadays the marriage union has become an economic partnership, where market rules other than sacrificial love are considered most important. But marriage is no game, or a commodity; it is a sacred commitment.

Although marriage is personal and intimate, it is also public. Engagements and weddings are public displays of your love and commitment, and warnings for all others to stay away from the union.

A good marriage is an asset to society. It ensures that children are born and raised to sustain future generations; and therefore any sexual immoralities that would jeopardize this goal can be considered counterintuitive.

Societies throughout the ages have placed a premium on good marriages. No society wants to deal with the nuances of a dysfunctional family, where problems spill over into the community, putting a strain on society's vital resources.

For example, when a baby is in the womb, nobody hopes the child will become transgendered, a lesbian, a prostitute, or the sex slave of a demonic spirit. In most cases, the aspiration is for the child to grow up and have a good marriage, and have children who will make a difference in society, to carry on the family traditions. Even those caught up in a dysfunctional family setting still hope the children will grow up to be different and lift up the honor of the family. Why then do people approve and support alternative marriages and lifestyles to undermine the family structure, to burden society? From the Bible:

> We know that the Law is spiritual; but I am a creature of the flesh [carnal, unspiritual], having been sold into slavery under [the control of] sin. For I do not understand my own actions [I am baffled, bewildered]. I do not practice or accomplish what I wish, but I do the very thing that I loathe [which my moral instinct condemns].                    (Roman 7:14-15 AMP)

It is all part of a spiritual scheme by Satan, to throw our relationships into chaos and to spiritually weaken and destabilize the world. But in the end, it would be said of Satan as written:

> Those who see you will gaze at you and consider you, saying, Is this the man who made the earth tremble, who shook kingdoms?--Who made the world like a wilderness and overthrew its cities, who would not permit his prisoners to return home?                    (Isaiah 14:16-17)

However, before then, it is imperative that we support key values and create an ideal environment, necessary for good marriages to thrive. But how do we recognize and nurture good marriages? Good marital relations are made, not born.

Marriage, like gardening, is not easy. It needs work, and protection. Only those who have sown good seeds in the marriage garden, and have patiently nurtured it, can expect to harvest its fruits. Any shortcut to circumvent the above is doomed to failure and undermines the family structure. From time to time, attend marriage seminars and if possible, invest time and money on marital counseling materials that are based on sound biblical, teachings.

The third ingredient needed to sustain the growth of the marriage garden is for the couple to seek and abide by the highest level of spirituality, consistent with the sacredness of their marriage vows.

When people make vows, they should not take them lightly. There are spiritual ramifications attached to those vows; they are not just empty words.

> When you make a vow to God, do not delay in fulfilling it. He has no pleasure in fools; fulfill your vow. It is better not to vow than to make a vow and not fulfill it.
> (Ecclesiastes 5:4-5 NIV)

> Marriage should be honored by all, and the marriage bed kept pure, for God will judge the adulterer and all the sexually immoral.
> (Hebrews 13:4 NIV)

When you follow spiritual rules as laid down by God, the Designer and Architect of family and marriage institutions, you set the tone and lay a strong foundation to ensure a successful marriage, where children are loved, disciplined, and nurtured into adults. They carry on the family traditions with honor and contribute to the good of society. When there is a divine presence in your family, no demonic agents can destroy your marriage. They may fight against you, but you will survive problems inherent in most marriages. To those who fear and obey God, His edicts have been issued:

> And you, be ye fruitful, and multiply; bring forth abundantly in the earth, and multiply therein. (Genesis 9:7)

> The LORD shall increase you more and more, you and your children. Ye are blessed of the LORD which made heaven and earth. (Psalm 115:14-15)

The above goals to maintain the marriage garden as I have listed may seem unachievable given the level of decadence in today's society. The reality is that, there are spiritual enforcers who have been assigned to bring to pass what is currently happening in our societies, and our world. The Word of God is truth, and does not lie. We are at war, and it is not against flesh and blood but against principalities, against powers, against the rulers of the darkness of this world, against spiritual wickedness in high places (Ephesians 6:12).

All of us have spiritual eyes and ears. But many are spiritually blind and deaf and therefore do not understand the implications of their actions. If marriage is a divine institution and good, why do people do things to break it up? What is inherent in man for the Bible to predict over two thousand years ago, the death of our relationships? What draw us together and what causes us to be unfaithful to each other? Is monogamy in marriage a myth? Is infidelity inevitable?

## Are We Wired to Cheat?

Based on the hurt, heartache, and havoc that infidelity has inflicted on many relationships, what makes cheating so attractive when so much is at stake? Why do couples still cheat in their marriage? What forces impact couples to disregard and break their sacred vows? It is all spiritual and yet hardly do you hear people discuss the spiritual ramifications of our relationships with one another. Infidelity is multifaceted and is part of a much bigger problem.

As a result of the fallen nature of man, the seeds of good and evil are embedded at the core of every human being. For example, sowing the seed of lust in one's heart can adversely impact the quality of his or her life. The attraction of lust is so powerful and yet often begins with innocuous sneaky second glances. On the physical level it may appear fun and harmless, but when captivated spiritually, when it has conquered or possessed your soul, it will enslave you to do its bidding.

Lust, just like sin, or any other social vice, because it is spiritually rooted, can be spiritually induced. Speaking of sin, God told Cain, "But if you do not do what is right, sin is crouching at your door; it desires to have you, but you must master it" (Genesis 4:7). We live in an age in which the desire of sin is everywhere.

We are the product of our environments. The barrage of sexual seductions, enticements, from environmental, technological, and other social stimuli have all contributed to an increased level of flagrant sensuality and, combined with our wicked hearts, have had an adverse impact on our lives and our communities. Everybody needs love, not lust. At the heart of most troubled relationships are various props and facades to mask the real spiritual deficiency in our love for one another, and towards the Almighty God, our Creator.

Are men more prone to cheating than women? I watched a *George Lopez* sitcom on TV in which a lady commented, "All men are cheaters." One gentleman replied, "I didn't cheat, my wife cheated on me." The lady laughed and said, "Because she is the man in the marriage." The spouse strongest in the spiritual realm is in control. CNN did a presentation on infidelity. It reported that a national survey, found that middle-aged couples today cheated at twice the rate of the generation before it. The CNN presentation also said:

> Whether you think cheating is unacceptable or inevitable, there's no denying one new trend: women are catching up with men. The trend with married women is that more married women are having extramarital intercourse. And so it looks like that gap is closing.
>
> (*CNN* Presents: Infidelity: Aired December 21, 2003).

Paul, commenting on the godlessness in the last days in his second letter to Timothy, said:

> BUT UNDERSTAND this, that in the last days will come (set in) perilous times of great stress and trouble [hard to deal with and hard to bear]. For people will be lovers of self and [utterly] self-centered, lovers of money and aroused by an inordinate [greedy] desire for wealth, proud and arrogant and contemptuous boasters. They will be abusive (blasphemous, scoffing), disobedient to parents, ungrateful, unholy and profane.
>
> (2 Timothy 3:1-2 AMP)

Paul's prediction is right on course. In the *CNN* presentation, an author with numerous adulterous relationships maintained that no one gets hurt as long as no one is caught, because what you don't know won't hurt you. However, if you are caught, *"The magic words, of course: deny, deny, deny."* This so-called expert said that only people who are odd or have zero self-esteem would consider having sex with one person forever. She is obviously from the school of thought that questions whether fidelity is even a realistic expectation for a marriage today, and believes that monogamy in marriage is a myth. Obviously, the message of the Gospel for these people has no meaning and is foolishness to the unregenerate heart.

The fact that people make decisions to cheat in their marriages does not mean everybody is cheating. In the Bible, during the time of the prophet Elijah, when everybody was into the worship of Baal, the sun god, Elijah complained to God:

> I have been very zealous for the LORD God Almighty. The Israelites have rejected your covenant, broken down your altars, and put your prophets to death with the sword. I am the only one left, and now they are trying to kill me too." [God said to Elijah] I reserve seven thousand in Israel--all whose knees have not bowed down to Baal and all whose mouths have not kissed him." (1 Kings 19:14, 18)

God is still in control, and He rules in the affairs of men. This universe belongs to God but there are still enemy territories in it. "We know [positively] that we are of God, and the whole world [around us] is under the power of the evil one" (1 John 5:19 AMP).

When people follow the dictates of their hearts, which the Bible describes as deceitful and desperately wicked (Jeremiah 17:9), they become prone to all kinds of foolishness and evil. Below are some Bible verses describing our hurting hearts--a common destiny for all:

> This is the evil in everything that happens under the sun: The same destiny overtakes all. The hearts of men, moreover, are full of evil and there is madness in their hearts while they live, and afterward they join the dead. (Ecclesiastes 9:3 NIV)

> For from within, [that is] out of the hearts of men, come base and wicked thoughts, sexual immorality, stealing, murder, adultery, Coveting (a greedy desire to have more wealth), dangerous and destructive wickedness, deceit; unrestrained (indecent) conduct; an evil eye (envy), slander (evil speaking, malicious misrepresentation, abusiveness), pride (the sin of an uplifted heart against God and man), foolishness (folly, lack of sense, recklessness, thoughtlessness). All these evil [purposes

and desires] come from within, and they make the man unclean
and render him unhallowed. (Mark 7:21-23 AMP)

Is this the same heart that psychoanalysts and other so-called sex experts advise people to follow? Don't be deceived. Instead listen to God. Many have followed the dictates of their hearts and have made bad choices by sowing the seed of evil. In the process, they have reaped nothing, but sorrow. Never compound your sorrows by taking advice from those who know nothing about the institution of holy matrimony as designed by God. Remember, the marriage union is a spiritual union. Don't neglect to seek spiritual help. Be careful of non-biblical advice, not all spiritual help is authentic. There are those who have made attempts to restore, nurture, and heal their broken relationships, yet these people are vilified for exemplifying the virtues of true sacrificial love. Those who know the Lord, and seek spiritual remedies to their problems, will sing out of joy from their hearts. But those who follow the dictates of their unspiritual hearts will cry from the anguish of their hearts and wail in brokenness of spirit according to Isaiah 65:14.

There is a well-orchestrated force of evil at work to destroy everything that is good and beautiful in your life. God's plans for your life are under attack. God's desire and plans for you to achieve a loving, lasting bond through family and marriage are facing an onslaught from the enemy. The devil is aware of the maxim, "United we stand, divided we fall" as per Ecclesiastes 4:12, so should you.

Spiritual forces have been assigned to ignite infighting among family units. No one marries with the intention of destroying his or her marriage. However, in the spiritual realm, it is altogether a different story. The devil invades people's lives and sows the seed of all sorts of devastation, the fruit of which we see manifested in the lives of his victims. The Bible therefore admonishes us to pray continually. You have to seek God and be fully committed to Him. If you take care of God's business, He will take care of your life, marriage, and family. Pray for others, but make sure you always pray for your marriage, family, and loved ones. When you intercede for them through your prayers, you stand in the gap for them spiritually.

## Triangular Love and Child Discipline

Children are the endearments of their parents. In a marriage, the children tend to bind the parents together in a triangular love. However, the devil seeks revenge by trying to corrupt them early. Since the seeds of our fallen nature are also found in our offspring, by nature they will disobey and test rules and boundaries, but discipline is the antidote that keeps a child from folly. Why does God insist we discipline our children?

> Foolishness is bound up in the heart of a child, but the rod of discipline will drive it far from him. (Proverbs 22:15 NIV)
>
> Discipline your children while you still have the chance; indulging them destroys them. (Proverbs 19:18 MSG)
>
> He who spares his rod [of discipline] hates his son, but he who loves him disciplines diligently and punishes him early. (Proverbs 13:24 AMP)
>
> You shall whip him with the rod and deliver his life from Sheol (Hades, the place of the dead). (Proverbs 23:14 AMP)
>
> Train a child in the way he should go, and when he is old he will not turn from it. (Proverbs 22:6 NIV)
>
> Wise discipline imparts wisdom; spoiled adolescents embarrass their parents. Discipline your children; you'll be glad you did-- they'll turn out delightful to live with. (Proverbs 29:15, 17 MSG)

In general, when God gives a command, it is for our protection. However, some people have decided that they are wiser than God. They are against parents disciplining their children by spanking when a child misbehaves. There is a difference between discipline and abuse, including humiliation, smacking, kicking, and punching.

These social scientists claim spanking is inhumane because the child will become psychologically and emotionally warped for life, and suffer low self-esteem. But in Hebrews we read:

> Now no chastening for the present seemeth to be joyous, but
> grievous: nevertheless afterward it yieldeth the peaceable fruit
> of righteousness unto them which are exercised thereby.
>
> (Hebrews 12:11)

When some critics don't like the message, they overly dwell on one issue they dislike thereby allowing it to cloud their judgment and in the process end up thrashing the messenger, or a book. The truth is that the human heart, including that of a child, is very wicked and rebellious, and therefore needs discipline, correction, and shepherding. I can't imagine Jesus beating a child, but God would warn a parent of the ramifications of the child's disobedience.

When God disciplines you, or the devil attacks you, the whole family suffers. Just ask Eli what transpired at Shiloh with regard to his inability to effectively discipline his two sons. God destroyed them.

No one likes being chastised or disciplined. But once a child understands the options that are available to his parents, it influences to some extent the way he behaves, all things being equal. But things are not always equal. Can a parent suffer and not the child? I have news for you. Just as a Christian can be influenced or tormented by evil spirits, so can a child. A rebellious ancestral spirit passed along generational lines can indwell a child in the form of a strong-willed child.

For those who don't want to deal with the hard choices of disciplining their children, including spanking when appropriate, be reminded that in God's book, corporal punishment is an option. However, the way it is administered would reveal the true state of a parent's heart. Many a parent's heart is broken because he or she failed to adhere to God's warnings and instructions with regard to childrearing, no matter how harsh it may be. God expects parents to discipline their children because God, as a parent, disciplines His children. He also disciplines people for their sins, including those of the fathers.

# Benjamin McLane Spock (The Book Says!)

When you rely on experts who encourage you to follow teachings contrary to the Word of God, the solutions to your problems will elude you. You'll look to the wrong places and rely on people who can't even help themselves. Dr. Benjamin Spock said spanking children is not good. His reassuring message to parents—that they should trust themselves as they attend to their children's physical and psychological needs geared toward a pleasurable domestic lifestyle. (Spock, Benjamin. *The Reader's Companion to American History.* http://college.hmco.com/history/readerscomp/rcah/html/ah_ 081200_spockbenjami.htm.) He said this at a time when the nation was preoccupied with children and family life, and it appealed to many. America hailed him as a pediatric guru. What happened to his grandchild? He committed suicide. *("Benjamin Spock, Physician Heal Thyself."* Vision Journal. Cited Nov. 2004. http://www.vision. org/jrnl/0006/bvbspock.html.)

The influences of the spiritual are for real. Dr. Spock relied on Sigmund Freud's earthly wisdom—man's paradigms over God's paradigms, and so at the end of his life it was said:

> Yet for all his compassionate advice to the mothers of the world, Spock mirrored his father's inability to give his own sons the love they needed. Grandson Peter's suicide and Spock's divorce after 48 years of marriage (because of his wife's repeated breakdowns, induced by alcoholism and medication abuse) shattered the image of the ideal family man.
>
> He saw the need for morals and values, but he failed to recognize that they stem from a godly perspective. What he never understood is that the positive changes he sought are simply unachievable on the basis of humanism.
> *("Benjamin Spock, Physician Heal Thyself."* Vision Journal. Cited November 2004. http://www.vision.org/jrnl/0006/bvbspock.html.*)

In Hebrews, we are reminded of the role of divine discipline (tough love).

> And have you [completely] forgotten the divine word of appeal

and encouragement in which you are reasoned with and addressed as sons?

My son, do not think lightly or scorn to submit to the correction and discipline of the Lord, nor lose courage and give up and faint when you are reproved or corrected by Him;

For the Lord corrects and disciplines everyone whom He loves, and He punishes, even scourges, every son whom He accepts and welcomes to His heart and cherishes.

(Hebrews 12:5-6 AMP)

The devil uses our lack of discipline and the overindulgence of our children against the family. When kids are hardly disciplined, they start calling the shots. The parents do whatever the children want. With no discipline at home, these kids have little tolerance for authority structure. They become arrogant, boastful, and brash. They grow up believing that the world is their oyster. In the end, what they cannot have they steal or kill to get. When we fail to discipline our children, their disrespects for authority become an open invitation for demonic spirits to afflict us if we neglect God's commandments to obey them. Many become miserable and despondent, and some even end up in jail.

As a child, I heard a story of a mother who overindulged her son. In the end, the law caught up with him and he ended up on death row. Before he was executed, he asked to talk to his mother. He asked her to come nearer as if to whisper in her ears. Suddenly, he bit off her ear, and said, "This is for not disciplining me and causing my downfall."

Other parents tend to be heavy-handed when it comes to disciplining their children. Parents often unleash their frustrations on the children. But the Bible warns against such tactics.

Fathers, do not irritate and provoke your children to anger [do not exasperate them to resentment], but rear them [tenderly] in the training and discipline and the counsel and admonition of the Lord.                                    (Ephesians 6:4)

In today's global village, the community rears the children without disciplining them. Who then disciplines and counsels them in the admonition of the Lord, the schools, the churches, or the states?

In the past, teachers were given permission to spank children, but today, parents have rescinded that authority. School board members have no choice but to comply or be slapped with lawsuits. Woe to the teacher who touches a student. No wonder our inner-city public schools have become a war zone. If we are not careful, there may come a time when teachers will need "combat allowance" to entice them to teach at inner-city problem schools.

The devil is using the concern for our children to fight against society by undermining our ability to effectively discipline them. Often, the devil plays one parent against the other, and the child is used as a pawn to undermine the authority at home. The results of our neglected responsibility to properly teach or discipline our children has brought us to a point where even the massacre at Columbine High School in Littleton, Colorado, and the rash of school shootings in rural areas such as Paducah, Kentucky; Jonesboro, Arkansas; and Conyers, Georgia; pale in comparison, to what the devil has in store to destabilize the home, and society at large, if God does not intervene.

Nothing happens by chance either spiritually or physically, so always be proactive with your children. This means anticipation, preparation, and sowing spiritual truths in their lives. For a lazy person who does not plow in season, come harvest time he will find nothing. According to the Bible, there is a time for every activity under the sun (Ecclesiastes 3:1). Get out of your comfort zone; be spiritually prepared and alert to what is happening in your life and your community. Do something, pray! Start praying for everybody because when the devil is finished with your neighbor it will be your turn. Besides individual prayers, corporate prayers are important. On your own, you become an easy target for the devil. When people pray together, things happen in the realm of the spirit. In Acts, we see the power of communal prayer in action.

It was about this time that King Herod arrested some who belonged

> to the church, intending to persecute them. He had James, the brother of John, put to death with the sword. When he saw that this pleased the Jews, he proceeded to seize Peter also. So Peter was kept in prison, but the church was earnestly praying to God for him.
>
> Suddenly an angel of the Lord appeared and a light shone in the cell. He struck Peter on the side and woke him up. "Quick, get up!" he said, and the chains fell off Peter's wrists. Then the angel said to him, "Put on your clothes and sandals." And Peter did so. "Wrap your cloak around you and follow me," the angel told him.
>
> When this had dawned on him, he went to the house of Mary the mother of John, also called Mark, where many people had gathered and were praying.          (Acts 12:1-3, 5, 7, 8, 12 NIV)

The devil tries to cause confusion by sowing the seed of discord to break our discipline and unity. Nowhere is this more prevalent than in the churches. Without adequate prayer power or covering, your spiritual wilderness could be cold, brutish, and nasty.

When you pray for your children, don't forget to pray for children in general as well. They are not only the future, they also part of the present. The devil will attack them while they are young because they are the ones who will grow up to become presidents, politicians, educators, lawmakers, and men of God.

Don't forget to pray for your community and nation. Nobody lives on an island. Someone's misfortune can touch you in a way that you did not anticipate. After all, you wouldn't want an evil spirit or a demon to enter into a neighborhood bully or the kid next door to introduce your children to cigarettes, occultism, sex, drugs, and alcohol, to break your heart, would you?

How would you like to see your politicians become so corrupt that no one's safety can be guaranteed? How would you feel if your president, and other leaders in your nation, enacted laws that infringe on your beliefs and ideals that have sustained the prosperity of your nation?

Finally, how would you like to see your pastors and church leaders become sexually immoral? When the shepherd of the flock has been discredited what happens to the message from the pulpit? You won't hear anything about sexual sins or immoralities because the spirit of Whoremonger hangs over the congregation like a wet blanket. When was the last time you checked the divorce statistics for the clergy? I am sure by now you understand why you have to pray not only for yourself, but also for everybody, even wicked people. Listen to what Paul said about praying for others. It may surprise you the first people we are to pray for.

> FIRST OF all, then, I admonish and urge that petitions, prayers, intercessions, and thanksgivings be offered on behalf of all men, For kings and all who are in positions of authority or high responsibility, that [outwardly] we may pass a quiet and undisturbed life [and inwardly] a peaceable one in all godliness and reverence and seriousness in every way.
>
> For such [praying] is good and right, and [it is] pleasing and acceptable to God our Savior, Who wishes all men to be saved and [increasingly] to perceive and recognize and discern and know precisely and correctly the [divine] Truth.
>
> For there [is only] one God, and [only] one Mediator between God and men, the Man Christ Jesus, Who gave Himself as a ransom for all [people, a fact that was] attested to at the right and proper time.                    (1 Timothy 2:1-6 AMP)

## Behavioral Science and Spirituality

What roles do science, religion, and spirituality play in our relationships? Is science and spirituality compatible? To me, science provides a tool or sheds light on what already exist. Before science, there was spirituality. However, there is room for both to coexist.

According to the Bible, there is nothing new under the sun. Everything will be discovered at the appropriate time, more so of spiritual things.

> The thing that has been--it is what will be again, and that

which has been done is that which will be done again; and
there is nothing new under the sun.

Is there a thing of which it may be said, See, this is new? It has
already been, in the vast ages of time [recorded or unrecorded]
which were before us.                    (Ecclesiastes 1:9-10 AMP)

In Daniel 12:4, we read that knowledge shall be increased. There
is no doubt that knowledge has increased, not only through the
proclamation of the Word of God, but also in the areas of science,
and medicine due to advances in technology. However, there are
those who have supplanted the Creator with science and claim there
is no God. They ridicule faith and make the Word of God a mockery.
They reject anything spiritual. This lie was first introduced by Satan
in the Garden, when he told Eve, "You will not surely die, for God
knows that when you eat of it your eyes will be opened, and you
will be like God, knowing good and evil" (Genesis 3:4-5). Implicit
in this assertion is the notion that men become the definer of what
is good and evil. As such, man in essence has become the measurer
and authority over all things. This sets us on a dangerous coalition
course with God's laws.

In the final analysis, there are no absolute truths. People decide what
is right or wrong based on what they feel is in their best interest.
Their willful rebellion and rejection of God correspond to their
physical reality. After all, they have become just like God, knowing
good and evil. Man's achievements bear testimony of this fallacy.

This same logic has found its way into the behavioral sciences.
There is no longer the realm of the spirit but self-empowerment,
and psychotherapy; therefore, we downplay the role and ability of
Satan or demonic spirits to influence the choices people make in
life as mere superstition. But over the centuries to today, people
offer worship or appeasements to different deities in hopes of better
lives.

Man operates on a tripartite dimension; the body (anatomy and
physiology), the soul (mind, will, and emotions), and the spirit
(the divine nature). Professionals who do not know the spiritual

dimension of the human species often lose sight of the important role spirituality plays in the life of an individual. No wonder most social scientists are befuddled at why certain therapies don't work or even worsen in some situations. For those locked in bad marriages, or who can't seem to find their true soul mates, there may be spiritual reasons for your predicaments.

One might ask, "Where is the accountability factor in our decision-making? Isn't there anything that happens to us because of the freewill choices we make, whether good or bad, without attributing them to God or the devil?" Sure, we make choices, but the truth is that in any outcome of a situation in our lives, are due to some things that are in our control, and other things that are out of our control. Spiritual influences can cause people to make bad choices. This brings us to the impact of behavioral sciences and spirituality on our decision-making processes.

Let's look at a situation where an individual's drinking problems have a negative impact on his marriage and family. The scientific mind-set would diagnose the negative physiological impact on the individual. Doctors would look at the body and determine the effects of alcohol on the limbic system and the resultant chemical imbalance in the brain. A review of the family history would perhaps reveal that alcoholism has been a hallmark problem for this family.

In the scientific realm, the why of the problem would be attributed to genetics, or perhaps an acquired behavior. Anyone born into this family would be labeled as susceptible to alcoholism. This may be so in the physical, but what about the realm of the spirit? As the problem gets worse and becomes chronic, no amount of medication or therapy can solve the problem. What alternate course of action is there for this individual, and the family?

Since alcoholism has been labeled as a disease, in the physical, the race for a cure stops with medication, and support groups. However, a person can easily relapse into his addiction and be worse off than before. Why? Addiction, just like recidivism can be spiritually induced. Have you ever looked for the spiritual principle behind recidivism? What causes people to be repeat offenders; be it wife beaters, uncontrolled rage, moral and social unacceptable behaviors, such as drug abuse, incarceration, or alcoholism?

Let's take for example the case of alcoholism. Spiritually, this is what happens. When the demon of alcoholism is kicked out, it tries to get back in when it finds there is no support, or faith fellowship to fill the void in his victim. If it succeeds, the fight for restoration will be seven times harder than before. The Lord Jesus, in Matthew confirmed this spiritual truth.

> When an evil spirit comes out of a man, it goes through arid places seeking rest and does not find it. Then it says, 'I will return to the house I left.' When it arrives, it finds the house unoccupied, swept clean and put in order. Then it goes and takes with it seven other spirits more wicked than itself, and they go in and live there. And the final condition of that man is worse than the first. That is how it will be "with this wicked ge neration."                    (Matthew 12:43-45)

The last statement holds so true for this great land. We as a nation have moved away from God and have become a wicked generation, greedy, self-seeking and dominated by evil. We see and experience more heinous crimes, on the sanctity of life and against institutions set by God. It will take a spiritual remedy to solve our problems.

Back to the example with alcoholism, those who only look at the physical tend to marginalize the importance of spiritual treatments. However, the person who becomes addicted to alcohol is in bondage to the demons of alcoholism. A review of the family may reveal a history of alcoholism. As demons of alcoholism are passed down along generational lines, they take over and control the family spiritually. Therefore, anybody who plays loose with alcohol easily becomes a victim. In fact, harder-to-break addictions correspond to stronger, wicked demons.

Sociopaths are made, not born. They are first made that way spiritually, when they become enslaved by wicked demons responsible for their conditions. You only see the handiwork of these demonic spirits in the physical, so any attempt to treat the problem without spiritual solutions may not succeed. That is why, in Hosea 4:6, God is worried that His people are perishing because of lack of knowledge. His people have gone into spiritual bondage, and so He laments:

> But this is a people plundered and looted, all of them trapped in pits or hidden away in prisons. They have become plunder, with no one to rescue them; they have been made loot, with no one to say, "Send them back."     (Isaiah 42:22 NIV)

There is no need for people to resign themselves to a state of hopelessness. Part, or all your answers can be found in the realm of the spirit. This is where the importance of waging spiritual warfare and the deliverance ministry come in handy. For treatment and restoration, people have to go to war to free captives from spiritual bondage, in order to achieve lasting peace and happiness, assuming they have become born again believers, indwelt by the Holy Spirit.

When it comes to our sexuality, sexual perverts may not necessarily be sociopaths. Many may be religious with strong ethical codes, but cannot control themselves. The demons of lust can open the door to other sexual promiscuities, which could lead to drugs, lies, cheating, insatiable sexual appetites, prostitution, homosexuality, and other social vises, even suicide, and murder.

For those who find themselves attached to any unsolicited spiritual unions, you and your partner will never solve your problems as long as there is a third party involved. Physical separation won't do it until you spiritually sever all relations with this entity, human or demonic, whatever it may be.

Psychologists and behavioral therapists on the other hand, have a neat package to explain spiritual phenomenon in psychoanalytic terms. For example, one such discipline believes that people are unconsciously attracted to mates who mirror the positive and negative traits in their parents with the hope that their partners will help them heal unresolved childhood pains. In essence your partner becomes your surrogate parent, and your marriage a therapy--where you become healed by the relationship. What I have described above is the theory behind the Imago Therapy of which Dr. Harville Hendrix is a leading proponent.

The solutions to our problems can first be found in the realm of the spirit and not in any unresolved childhood pains, as psychoanalysts would have us believe. Our relational problems pre-date childhood deviations. Is marriage therapeutic? Yes of course marriage is therapeutic, because it carries a divine mandate. Marriage is a spiritual as well as a physical union. It is through marriage and the family that God chose to populate the earth. They are the institutions by which God's chosen people are raised here on earth.

Rather unfortunately, these are the same institutions by which the devil also works through the children of disobedience to achieve his purpose here on earth. No wonder our relationships are in such turmoil. There are many inherent mysteries in marriage and only those who have sought answers from the God of the Bible; architect of the marriage and family institutions would find its meaning, intricacies, challenges and blessings.

For those who have sought and tried counseling, support groups, step programs, books and tapes, yet none of these have helped, it doesn't mean you are doing something wrong. Support networks have their place in the process of recovery for abusive spousal relationships, but all these belong to the second part of the solution. Seek first a spiritual solution, and all others will follow. However, people seek spiritual help when all else have failed.

The sciences may explain the "what" and "how" of a phenomenon, however, external programs can have positive and lasting results if they are based upon the central truth that only God can restore peace, and joy in a spiritually depraved home. Any therapeutic help devoid of spiritual underpinnings can, at best, only alleviate the symptoms of the problem. No external help can achieve true peace until there is an inner repentance, and spiritual regeneration of the heart, and mind. If you are a Christian and have been seeking help from non-biblical sources for your problems, beware. God laments:

> For My people have committed two evils: they have forsaken
> Me, the Fountain of living waters, and they have hewn for
> themselves cisterns, broken cisterns which cannot hold water.
> (Jeremiah 2:13 AMP)

God is the one who can truly change an addict or an abusive partner, and at the same time "re-wire" the mind of the aggrieved spouse to bring wholeness and harmony to the home.

## Fatal Attraction

Couples who have similar love styles tend to last longer. However, don't let the lust of your eyes deceive you. People don't come into your life by chance. They come for a reason. Be careful of suitors who come to sweep you off your feet. They come in the form of those who just want to play, or portray themselves as larger-than-life, the "power players" as they are called. There are also the "schmoozers" who are nothing more than users, who travel in high-profile social circles and exploit their associations with the rich and famous.

Have you ever wondered why certain women are attracted to the wrong men? Or why children behave similar to the way their parents behaved? For example, whatever these children saw their parents do to resolve conflict is what they will do if faced with a similar situation. Why do you think children of dysfunctional parents tend to grow up to be abusive parents? Dysfunctional children from broken homes may have curses operating in their lives, because of demonic covenants that exist in the family. The demonic spirits that were controlling the parents tend to also follow these children. We all know that with children, training is important. However, how do we account for children who come from good homes but are still attracted to the wrong elements? What will happen to the marriage or family relationships of these children? Always look for answers in the realm of the spirit.

Spiritually, the marriages of children may have been sold even before they started dating. As adults, when they are looking for intimacy but are impatient, and don't seek the face of the Lord, they become vulnerable to enticements from the devil. He sets them up by throwing demons of loneliness at them, and at the same time sends contrary agents into their lives to victimize them. Without spiritual fortitude, the women succumb to good-for-nothing men who abuse them. They become attracted to liars, men who are selfish, full of rage, greedy, jealous, possessive, egotistical, wicked, insensitive, domineering, and plain evil to make their lives a living hell. As long as the spiritual dimension of a problem is not recognized and dealt with at its spiritual roots, there will always be broken relationships.

Take a careful look at the relationships of your favorite stars at Hollywood, and you would discover that all that glitters is not gold. Good training, money, and connections alone cannot save a marriage, if the spiritual foundation of a relationship is weak, faulty, or all together missing. The façade of good jobs, impressive clothes, luxury cars, expensive jewelry, and mansions cannot often hide the heartache that a spouse may be going through. Why this fatal attraction? Ladies, if you refuse to seek the face of the Lord and wait on Him, the devil will send his "Prince Charming" into your life to turn your world upside down. Trust in God because:

> It is of the LORD's mercies that we are not consumed, because his compassions fail not. They are new every morning: great is thy faithfulness.

> The LORD is my portion, saith my soul; therefore will I hope in him. The LORD is good unto them that wait for him, to the soul that seeketh him.

> It is good that a man should both hope and quietly wait for the salvation of the LORD. It is good for a man that he bear the yoke in his youth. (Lamentations 3:22-27)

Youthful lust is a powerful delirium. Men are not immune from making bad choices either. Those who follow outward beauty, without prayerfully considering the inner attributes of a potential partner, can easily fall prey to contrary agents to make their lives a nightmare. Some of the most attractive people have the ugliest, most despicable attitudes and personalities imaginable. This too is the work of the enemy and is therefore spiritually induced! The enmity between the seed of the serpent and that of the woman still rages on.

It is no coincidence that there is a world system out there that glamorizes the degradation of women through music and movies, where women are seen as sex objects to arouse the sexual lust of men, to further fuel an already explosive promiscuous environment. Women who resist often pay the price for their "insolence," through emotional, psychological, or physical abuse. They are made to feel that it is their fault, and they brought it upon themselves. These women saw the same thing happen to their parents, yet can't seem to break this vicious cycle of abuse.

Why do you think children of dysfunctional parents tend to grow up to be abusive parents? It all starts in the realm of the spirit. As more abusive spirits begin to follow these children, the girls are themselves abused by other children at a much younger age as they begin to date. By the time they are ready to marry, even those who have been taught to identify the red flags and symptoms of an abusive relationship still face the insidious problems of emotional and psychological abuses.

There is a popular saying that love is blind. Yes, only to those who don't understand the differences between the inner beauties of love, and the outer deceptions of lust, and so it said that only fools fall in love. The true Christian does not fall but descends in love and is therefore, not blindsided by lust. True love is spiritual and comes down from God because God is love according to 1 John 4:7-8.

The soul of people can be knit together, and so people should be careful of their former lovers, business partners of the opposite sex, and even their Christian brothers or sisters who may be impacting the marriage relationship in a negative way. Evil spirits delight in causing confusion. Any manifestations of demonic entities to interfere in the marriage union could cause a provocation, either through the male, or female, or even a third party to doom the marriage. To avoid confusion and mistrust, a man should not shower favors at another woman, not even at his Christian sister, at the expense of his wife.

## The Alpha Male

We live in a society where we glamorize sports personalities for their competitiveness. We admire their desire to excel on the field. We put these athletes on a pedestal. But have you ever thought of what the pent-up aggression, the competitiveness, the desire to be in control, and the need to dominate opponents do to these poor souls outside the realm of sports?

Fame, money, and power make these people surround themselves with an air of invincibility. Sooner or later this sense of invincibility is put to the test as opportunities arise and temptations by the demons of power, pride, arrogance, chauvinism, meanness, disrespect, boastfulness, lust, lies, ego, intimidation, taunting, stinginess, coercion, self-indulgence, sex, drugs, and alcohol come knocking at their doors.

Those who are not spiritually, emotionally, and physically prepared to handle fame and fortune become shackled. They often wind up in prison, in rehab, or dead. Those with good role models and mentoring figures are able to deal with their alpha male natures, as long as they tap into a support group or faith fellowship.

When something happens in the physical, certain aspects of it can be traced to the spiritual realm. We read in the Bible where Jesus encountered the demon-possessed man of Gadara. This man had at least two thousand demons residing in him.

> When Jesus stepped ashore, he was met by a demon-possessed man from the town. For a long time this man had not worn clothes or lived in a house, but had lived in the tombs.
>
> When he saw Jesus, he cried out and fell at his feet, shouting

at the top of his voice, "What do you want with me, Jesus, Son of the Most High God? I beg you, don't torture me!" For Jesus had commanded the evil spirit to come out of the man.

Many times it had seized him, and though he was chained hand and foot and kept under guard, he had broken his chains and had been driven by the demon into solitary places.

Jesus asked him, "What is your name?" "Legion," he replied, because many demons had gone into him. And they begged him repeatedly not to order them to go into the Abyss.

(Luke 8:27-31)

Can demons inhabit or influence a Christian? You bet! If you are a Christian and you are living unrighteously without genuinely confessing your sins, you become fair game to evil spirits. Don't toy with the devil or you will end up being his toy. The presence of one demon may open the door to others more vile and perverse than the first, and close the door to good advice and sound judgment.

To all the "Alphas" out there, don't play loose with your life by playing "Prince Charming" with the women, and don't invite the demons of power or lust to your spiritual arena for a game, for you will surely lose. They will enslave, torment, hurt and disgrace you. Ask the Indiana Pacers basketball team of 2004, about the fallout of "Alpha" traits, at the Motor City (Detroit) and they will tell you, it was costly and bad for team sports. Be careful, uncontrolled temper can be costly.

A patient man has great understanding, but a quick-tempered man displays folly. Better a patient man than a warrior, a man who controls his temper than one who takes a city.

(Proverbs 14:29; 16:32 NIV)

Women are effective bait against men. In the Garden of Eden, the devil and the woman were in cahoots to set up the man. Be careful of the trap of the enemy or else he will set you up spiritually.

Ask Kobe Bryant and he would tell you that he didn't do anything wrong, that it was consensual sex. Sure it was consensual at other times until, at the right time, his accuser was introduced into his life. The monetary cost to appease his wife and his legal cost were no peanuts. What about the spiritual cost to all parties involved in the case? Be vigilant of the devil's sensual and sexual baits, and don't get caught in his traps. Here is some advice from the Bible:

> Do not lust in your heart after her beauty or let her captivate you with her eyes, for the prostitute reduces you to a loaf of bread, and the adulteress preys upon your very life. Can a man scoop fire into his lap without his clothes being burned? Can a man walk on hot coals without his feet being scorched?
> (Proverbs 6:25-28)

> Whoever is simple (wavering and easily led astray), let him turn in here! And as for him who lacks understanding, she says to him, Stolen waters (pleasures) are sweet [because they are forbidden]; and bread eaten in secret is pleasant. But he knows not that the shades of the dead are there [specters haunting the scene of past transgressions], and that her invited guests are [already sunk] in the depths of Sheol (the lower world, Hades, the place of the dead). (Proverbs 9:16-18 AMP)

When God gives you riches, He does not interfere with how you use them. It is up to you whether you use them to glorify Him, or Self.

## Gentlemen, Our Manhood is under Spiritual Attack

God designed the male to be the authority figure in a family. Men, therefore, instinctively feel out of control and become agitated when their manhood comes under attack. Some lash out at their women out of weakness. This bad is for the marriage. It is also detrimental to the entire family because they have struck a blow for the devil.

It is not by accident that we are seeing a more rapid blurring of gender roles contrary to God's original design and purpose. The Bible says Satan is the god of this world, so we had better wake up to the trend of things in the world. The reversal of gender roles is a spiritual phenomenon and a physical reality. There is no doubt that we are in the end times and mystical Babylon is hard at work to elevate women and relegate men to subservient positions. In times to come, we will see many women in prominent positions of power in government, business, churches, and in families. If we allow events in people's lives to pass without connecting them to spiritual issues, we risk waking up one day and wondering, "How did this happen?"

The strategy of the devil is to destroy the family structure. To accomplish this, he indirectly undermines our manhood by fighting against our financial prosperity. In the future we may have to look at the definition of manhood because just wearing pants will not be enough for a man to be the head of his household. The woman, or wife could be calling the shots if she is the breadwinner. In a world where the yardstick of human success and power is measured by material wealth, masculinity without financial muscle, or education, is meaningless. Our authority may erode thereby upsetting the traditional family structure as instituted by God.

An article appeared in the *New Jersey Star Ledger* titled, *"Where the Boys Aren't"* which gives an insightful look at the problem. It says:

> Some experts in higher education are sounding the alarm about the college gender-gap, predicting a crisis that will affect every aspect of society. Men will get less education and money, jeopardizing the economy and leaving highly educated women without mates of similar status. Some believe American boys and men are in trouble, with rising rates of suicide and incarceration, and higher rates of learning disabilities or behavior problems.
> (Peggy O'Crowley. *The Sunday Star Ledger*-September 14, 2003)

The seemingly innocuous power struggle between genders can even be seen in the education system. Some experts believe we have to look at the problem from its roots, starting with an assessment of how we educate little boys, in order to change the course of male development.

However, advocates for women welcome the change in favor of girls. They claim the rules have changed in a society where things naturally went to men. Nowadays many women are making more money than their male partners, which is not bad per se. However, in a subtle way this can undermine the authority at home because it infringes on the traditional role of the man and woman within the matrimonial setting. The man is not able to rule over his home as God has decreed (Genesis 3:16; Colossians 3:18).

Marriage is not a fifty-fifty deal or partnership. However, it can be problematic where the man is not able to fulfill his role as the breadwinner of the family, and for the woman to take care of the house. There is resentment if the woman works outside the home, comes in tired, and still has to do all the household chores, while the man is perceived as not doing his fair share of maintaining the house. This is particularly true of the western culture, as found in industrialized nations.

For men, the devil likes to attack our egos by hitting where it hurts most; our finances. Therefore, in a materialistic society, where power is based on economics, the partner short on cash, who does not produce, is seen as the weaker vessel. In the end, the relationship becomes a power struggle with origins from the realm of the spirit.

Gentlemen, no matter your financial situation, you must not give up your birthright as the spiritual head of your family. In God's eyes, the wife is not the spiritual head of the household when there is a man around. Don't become like Esau, who relinquished his birthright to Jacob. Gentlemen:

> Watch out for the Esau syndrome: trading away God's lifelong
> gift in order to satisfy a short-term appetite. You well know
> how Esau later regretted that impulsive act and wanted God's
> blessing--but by then it was too late, tears or no tears.
>                                         (Hebrews 12:16-17 MSG)

God has decreed that the desire of the woman would be for her husband (Genesis 3:16), so to those who may be experiencing financial hardships and other marital problems, my advice is, don't resort to various forms of emotional, psychological, and physical abuses or assaults on your spouse. It is wrong and also a sign of weakness and loss of control. Instead, ask God to intervene in your situation and to deliver you from all the anti-prosperity forces fighting against your life. These spiritual forces include the spirits of want and poverty, envy, greed, insatiable appetite, anxiety, fear, hopelessness, worthlessness, depression, anger or rage, and perhaps even murder-suicide.

Some women, in an attempt to fulfill their divine role, in support of their men, find themselves in abusive situations. Some succeed in breaking away from the relationship. However, those who wait too long in seeking help end up enduring more abuse than necessary, and at times, pay the ultimate price. Men who commit these atrocities end up being incarcerated, to further weaken the family.

Seek the face of God and ask Him to fix your life and marriage. Ask Him to protect and help you avoid temptations. He who has promised is faithful and He will do it.

## Every Home Needs a Father Figure

> See, I will send you the prophet Elijah before that great and dreadful day of the LORD comes. He will turn the hearts of the fathers to their children, and the hearts of the children to their fathers; or else I will come and strike the land with a curse.
>
> (Malachi 4:5-6 NIV)

Men are always needed in the home or family but in America, no groups of people have suffered more than in the African-American communities, where a disproportionate number of black men make up the prison population. *(Prison," Microsoft® Encarta® Online Encyclopedia 2005 http://encarta.msn.com © 1997-2005 Microsoft Corporation).*

You cannot substitute female for male or vice versa, that is why in the beginning God created male and female. A man and woman make a family in God's eye and children are His blessings and reward.

We are becoming a nation of single-parent families, with women raising children by themselves. The men who could help mentor the kids have become absentee fathers. The absenteeism may not be necessarily physical but emotional, as well as spiritual. Women alone, cannot do the job barring other mentoring alternatives that can help teach these kids right from wrong, or pass down the mantle of leadership to subsequent generations. In the Bible, we see instances of mentorship between Moses and Joshua, Samuel and David, Elijah and Elisha, Jesus and the twelve disciples, and Paul and Timothy.

Mentorship not only has benefits but blessings as well. Mentorship is about receiving and passing down family traditions, principles, and truths capable of sustaining the human race. God instituted multigenerational family relations to smoothly help pass down His laws to subsequent generations. God has embedded mentorship in each one of us. As Christians, we lose our sense of history, and spiritual identity when we neglect to avail ourselves of this God-given provision for our spiritual growth. Without this mentoring process, we effectively undermine God's command to teach His statutes to our children, and they to their children to avoid falling prey to the devil.

Some may think they don't need a father figure or a mentor, but without a good role model who has nurtured and raised you, where are you going get first hand training in order to pass them on to your children? If you bring a child into this world, it is your duty to take care of that child. For those without fathers, and grew up under the shadow of a mother or grandmother, the fact that you were neglected by your father during childhood should be an extra incentive and a challenge to break the cycle and do the right thing. Don't be mean to your children. Their angels are watching, according to Matthew 18:10.

Gentlemen, our manhood over the years has come under increasing spiritual attacks, and as a result some people have either consciously or unconsciously shunned their responsibilities to care for their children. These men have denied their children a father figure, which is critical in any family setting. God will hold you responsible if you neglect your children and do not provide for them--not only with food, clothing, and shelter, but also emotional, psychological, and spiritual support. Without love or nurturing from the father, the spiritual bond and blessings become depleted and inadequate in the child's life. These children seek love and attention elsewhere. Sometimes the girls grow up thinking they don't need to marry to have children. They don't see the need for a husband but God did not design the family to include cohabitation.

The teenage years are critical developmental milestones in the life of a child. As the youth grow up, their needs and desires change, as well as those of their mates. When these people rush into relationships before they have matured and are ready to marry, the marriage often does not succeed. The devil knows that young men have strong sexual urges, so he uses that to distort their judgments. In 2 Timothy the Bible warns us to:

> Shun youthful lusts and flee from them, and aim at and pursue righteousness (all that is virtuous and good, right living, conformity to the will of God in thought, word, and deed); [and aim at and pursue] faith, love, [and] peace (harmony and concord with others) in fellowship with all [Christians], who call upon the Lord out of a pure heart. (2 Timothy 2:22 AMP)

In 2004, Bill Cosby, a comedian and philanthropist, tried to engage African-Americans in a social dialogue. Some of his own people took offense at his message of social responsibility, and of parents being accountable for the well-being of their children. They claimed he was missing the point. To these people, the real problem lie with the socio-economic system that has relegated many to second-class citizens, deprived of the resources to maintain their families and become productive citizens. The heart and soul of the matter is that there is a heavenly Father who is interested in the well being of His children. How many people have sought spiritual remedies to their economic and political woes? How many people believe that God still rules in the affairs of men?

From Bill Cosby's perspective, any meaningful transformation must first begin with a deep soul-searching of the family. It is written:

> If anyone fails to provide for his relatives, and especially for
> those of his own family, he has disowned the faith [by failing to
> accompany it with fruits] and is worse than an unbeliever [who
> performs his obligation in these matters].
>
> (1 Timothy 5:8 AMP)

Provision for the family does not necessarily mean bread and butter, but also moral guidance. Parents should be good role models to their children and not depend on others to teach them moral values. When you instill discipline in your children and teach them to take responsibility for their actions, they will learn to take care of themselves, and not blame society for their failures. Charity (love) begins at home. Even though your family may not have enough, "Better is little with the fear of the LORD than great treasure and trouble therewith," according to Proverbs 15:16. Dependence on an institution will not save us as a people, but our love for one another, rooted in the fear of God, will. Can I hear an amen?

The devil has always incited people to shoot down the messenger if they don't appreciate the message. So, like missionaries of old who braved the dangers of the new world, to bring the gospel of Jesus Christ, the gospel of love, peace, and the offer of life eternal, today we need people who will stand up just like those brave souls did and give a spiritual voice to what is happening in our society before it is too late. Your love and concern for those who are perishing, who are experiencing relational troubles at work or in their marriages and families, should galvanize you to share the good news of the gospel of Jesus Christ. For these reasons we are to:

> Preach the Word; be prepared in season and out of season;
> correct, rebuke and encourage--with great patience and careful
> instruction.                         (2 Timothy 4:2 NIV)

The spiritual realm is real. What you don't know will hurt you. But how do you defend against what you can't see? Inquiring minds should be like the Bereans who read the Bible in search of the truth (Acts 17:11). Seek the truth, and the truth shall set you free according to John 8:32.

# Avoid Verbal Jabs and Demon Talk

> But if instead of showing love among yourselves you are
> always biting and devouring one another, watch out! Beware of
> destroying one another.                    (Galatians 5:15 NLT)

> Rebuke not an elder, but entreat him as a father; and the younger
> men as brethren; the elder women as mothers; the younger as
> sisters, with all purity.                    (1 Timothy 5:1-3)

Don't be disrespectful to your elders. Stop calling women foul names, and avoid using profanity and derogative remarks in your language.  There is life and death in the power of the tongue. Your killer words can uproot and tear down, destroy and overthrow people emotionally, psychologically, and spiritually.

Keep telling your child that he is a moron, and he is going to grow up believing that he is worthless. You planted that seed in him when he was a child.  You have a choice of words. Choose words that build, implant, and empower life, words that generate peace and harmony, words such as "I love you, I adore you, I affirm and appreciate you. I'm always there for you. You can count on me." Your spouse and your children need to hear those words from you all the time.

A friend of mine was telling me about some issues he was having with his wife. She would say mean and nasty things to him. Whenever he opened his mouth to defend himself, she would smack him and tell him, "You hit me and I will have the cops lock you up." I told him to disregard the "demon talk" and be patient, knowing that we are not fighting against flesh and blood, but spiritual wickedness.

Competition in marriage can be very destructive. It invites the devil to interfere in your affairs. To avoid serious fallouts, the Bible warns in Ephesians, "When angry, do not sin; do not ever let your wrath (your exasperation, your fury or indignation) last until the sun goes down. Leave no [such] room or foothold for the devil [give no opportunity to him] (Ephesians 4:26-27 AMP). When squabbles are spiritually induced, some people say hurtful things to their spouses.

One thing leads to another, and before they know it, the insult has spread to the rest of the family. Sometimes the couple can resolve their differences, but what about the aggrieved parties outside the marriage? Don't let verbal jabs become knockout or killer punches to defile your spouse and entire family. The Bible warns us to avoid anything that could cause bitterness to defile many. We are warned:

> Exercise foresight and be on the watch to look [after one another], to see that no one falls back from and fails to secure God's grace (His unmerited favor and spiritual blessing), in order that no root of resentment (rancor, bitterness, or hatred) shoots forth and causes trouble and bitter torment, and the many become contaminated and defiled by it--.
>
> (Hebrews 12:15 AMP)

If a spiritual dimension is not factored into any conflict-resolution process, the marriage could eventually come to a halt, with untold sufferings for all the parties involved. The broken home will be reported in the satanic kingdom as "mission accomplished." This normally happens with the aid of household witchcraft, members of your own family who are agents of the enemy. The sad part of it is that all these family members are themselves victims or collateral damages in the prevailing spiritual warfare.

In the realm of the spirit a domineering, and controlling wife may be the "man" in a marriage. She is made that way by household witchcraft. When that happens, there is endless power struggle in the marriage because there can be only one "true king,"--either the husband, designated by God to be the head of the household, or the wife, designated by witchcraft (the Jezebel spirit) to be the "man" in the marriage. You lose the spiritual battle when you abuse or beat up your wife. Instead use spiritual warfare prayers. Do you know how to defend yourself? Is your lifestyle incongruent with your calling? Are your ancestors under a curse? If you are a Christian, you have been given the power to fight back because Jehovah Elohim, (the Creator of heaven and earth), the master Architect of the family and marriage institutions is on your side. As Lord of Host, and Lord of your life, He will fight for you.

All marriages go through some sort of turmoil. If your relationship is on life support, or embroiled in endless power struggles, seek divine help. When there is a problem in a marriage, the Christian looks to Jesus, the Author and Perfector of his or her faith, to remain faithful to the union. Listen to the words of Jesus, Lover of your soul:

> Come to Me, all you who labor and are heavy-laden and overburdened, and I will cause you to rest. [I will ease and relieve and refresh your souls.]
>
> Take My yoke upon you and learn of Me, for I am gentle (meek) and humble (lowly) in heart, and you will find rest (relief and ease and refreshment and recreation and blessed quiet) for your souls.
>
> For My yoke is wholesome (useful, good--not harsh, hard, sharp, or pressing, but comfortable, gracious, and pleasant), and My burden is light and easy to be borne.
>
> (Matthew 11:28-30 AMP)

Verbal jabs are nothing but "demon talk" to sow seeds of resentment, generating unnecessary conflicts that lead to unhappiness, devastation, destruction, and the death of your relationship. Even if you are right, there is no gain in antagonizing your partner. You must realize that your loved one is more important than the issue under dispute. It is good and pleasant for brothers to dwell in unity. This is God's will for our lives as stated in Psalm 133:1.

The good news is that although there are spiritual forces determined to ruin our lives, God has not left us defenseless. That is why there are rules in every society to ensure that people live in peace. God has embedded in every human being the ethics of reciprocity and other guidelines for our daily living. Every culture on earth understands and practices, to some extent, the sacred concepts embodied in the Golden Rule, which says, "Do unto others as you would have them do unto you." To survive your marriage, follow these two commands:

> Love the Lord your God with all your heart and with all your soul and with all your strength and with all your mind"; and,
> Love your neighbor as yourself.          (Luke 10:27 NIV)

Remember, the big lie from the devil is to make you feel that there is a lot more that divides you than what you have in common with your partner or loved one.

## Honor Thy Father and Mother

The fifth command of the Ten Commandments comes with a promise. In Ephesians we read:

> Children, obey your parents in the Lord, for this is right. "Honor your father and mother"--which is the first commandment with a promise--"that it may go well with you and that you may enjoy long life on the earth." (Ephesians 6:1-3 NIV)

The grand design of the devil is to have children rebel against their parents, to lose not only their spiritual protection but also their blessings. Without spiritual covering, your children will easily fall prey to any evil influences the devil throws at society to enslave them. They could also become agents of the devil to influence societal trends. The devil will turn them against you, and they will spurn your love.

First, they may become selfish and ungrateful to their parents. In 1 Samuel, when the Israelites asked for a king, below is what God told the prophet Samuel.

> And the LORD told him: "Listen to all that the people are saying to you; it is not you they have rejected, but they have rejected me as their king. He said, "This is what the king who will reign over you will do:
>
> He will take your sons and make them serve with his chariots and horses, and they will run in front of his chariots. Some he will assign to be commanders of thousands and commanders of fifties, and others to plow his ground and reap his harvest, and still others to make weapons of war and equipment for his chariots.

He will take your daughters to be perfumers and cooks and bakers. He will take the best of your fields and vineyards and olive groves and give them to his attendants. He will take a tenth of your grain and of your vintage and give it to his officials and attendants.

Your menservants and maidservants and the best of your cattle and donkeys he will take for his own use.

He will take a tenth of your flocks, and you yourselves will become his slaves. When that day comes, you will cry out for relief from the king you have chosen, and the LORD will not answer you in that day." (1 Samuel 8:7, 11-18 NIV)

The above is a spiritual representation of what happens when a nation or a person rejects Jesus Christ as the King of their lives. According to the Bible:

Salvation is found in no one else, for there is no other name under heaven given to men by which we must be saved. For there [is only] one God, and [only] one Mediator between God and men, the Man Christ Jesus.

(Acts 4:12; 1 Timothy 2:5 AMP)

Yet for us there is [only] one God, the Father, Who is the Source of all things and for Whom we [have life], and one Lord, Jesus Christ, through and by Whom are all things and through and by Whom we [ourselves exist]. I am the Way and the Truth and the Life; no one comes to the Father except by (through) Me.

(1 Corinthians 8:6 AMP; John 14:6 AMP)

For those who think there are other ways, hear the claim by Jesus that He is the only mediator between God and man. Either Jesus was telling the truth, or He was a lunatic or a liar. Find out for yourself. This is the discovery Philip shared with Nathanael:

Philip found Nathanael and told him, "We have found the one Moses wrote about in the Law, and about whom the prophets also wrote--Jesus of Nazareth, the son of Joseph."

(John 1:45 NIV)

Those who reject Jesus become an instrument of change in the

156

hands of the devil. Your sons and daughters will belong to him and they will be his slaves. He will steal your blessings; he will kill and destroy your life. Your daughters could turn to prostitution and become the wives and sex slaves of evil spirits who will become the third parties in their marriages. When that happens, their marriages won't last, and there will always be strife in their homes.

He will lock their wombs or afflict them with infertility and rob them of the joy of motherhood. For men, maintaining a state of fidelity and monogamy would be tenuous at best. He will touch their finances, get them in debt, or afflict them with greed and an insatiable appetite for money instead of Jesus, the true spiritual nourishment of our souls and spirits. These people will become their own gods. Whatever charitable services they engage in, their best deeds of rightness and justice are nothing but filthy rags in the eyes of God, according to Isaiah 64:6.

The United States of America was founded on Judeo-Christian principles, which have sustained the nation until now. Yet in America today, we have agreed to kick anything related to religion, and God out of the classroom in favor of multi-pluralism. However, when there is national disaster, people suddenly become religious. Spirituality, not religion, is the answer.

Today in America, we have the most religious freedom of any country in the world, including the freedom to believe or not to believe in divine authority. Throughout history, man has had choices. We as a nation are faced with the same options Joshua put before ancient Israel:

> But if serving the LORD seems undesirable to you, then choose
> for yourselves this day whom you will serve, whether the gods
> your forefathers served beyond the River, or the gods of the
> Amorites, in whose land you are living. But as for me and my
> household, we will serve the LORD.     (Joshua 24:15 NIV)

Anne Graham Lotz, the second daughter of the great evangelist Billy Graham, commenting on the 9/11/01 tragedy, gave a profound and insightful response as to why there is so much turmoil in our midst today. During an interview on the *Early Show,* Jane Clayson asked, "I've heard people say,--those who are religious, those who are not--, if God is good, how could God let this happen? To that, you say?" Anne Graham Lotz replied, "I say God is also angry when he sees something like this. I would say also for several years now Americans in a sense have shaken their fist at God and said, God, we want you out of our schools, our government, our business, we want you out of our marketplace. And God, who is a gentleman, has just quietly backed out of our national and political life, our public life. Removing his hand of blessing and protection." *(CBS News. Early Report (Early Show) Where Is God. September 13, 2001.* To a sinful nation, hear the Words of the Almighty God:

> "Woe to the obstinate children," declares the LORD, "to those who carry out plans that are not mine, forming an alliance, but not by my Spirit, heaping sin upon sin";     (Isaiah 30:1 NIV)

When God withdraws His protection, people become fair game, and the devil steps in to administer all kinds of affliction and devastation as written:

> All who found them devoured them; and their adversaries said, We are not guilty, because they have sinned against the Lord [and are no longer holy to Him], their true habitation of righteousness and justice, even the Lord, the hope of their fathers.
> (Jeremiah 50:7 AMP)

It has become politically correct to propagate profanity and indecency in the name of free speech, to murder unborn children in the name of pro-choice, to be covetous and greedy in the name of ambition, and to be sacrilegious and immoral in the name of tolerance.

When we compromise on either the good, the bad, or the ugly in order to be politically correct, this nation will become its own worst enemy. To any person or nation that turns away from God, and trivializes things that belong to Him, hear this solemn decree.

> I will return to My place [on high] until they acknowledge their

offense and feel their guilt and seek My face; in their affliction
and distress they will seek, inquire for, and require Me earnestly
.                                          (Hosea 5:15 AMP)

# Separation and Divorce

Divorce, just like spiritual divorce is symbolic of hell on earth.
Divorce tears apart our relationship with one another and the
marriage meant to symbolize our absolute spiritual union with God.
Do you really want to know how God feels about separation and
divorce? God hates divorce.

> For the Lord, the God of Israel, says: I hate divorce and marital
> separation and him who covers his garment [his wife] with
> violence. Therefore keep a watch upon your spirit [that it may
> be controlled by My Spirit], that you deal not treacherously and
> faithlessly [with your marriage mate].     (Malachi 2:16 AMP)

God did not intend the family, the building block of society to fall
apart. Separation and divorce have resulted because of sin, because
of our selfishness and disobedience. The Bible says that divorce
came about because of the stubbornness of our hearts. When the
Pharisees wanted to trap Jesus on the thorny issue of divorce and
separation base on what Moses had said, Jesus reminded them:

> And he answered and said unto them, Have ye not read, that
> he which made them at the beginning made them male and
> female, And said, For this cause shall a man leave father and
> mother, and shall cleave to his wife: and they twain shall be one
> flesh? Wherefore they are no more twain, but one flesh. What
> therefore God hath joined together, let not man put asunder.
>
> They say unto him, Why did Moses then command to give
> a writing of divorcement, and to put her away? He saith unto
> them, Moses because of the hardness of your hearts suffered
> you to put away your wives: but from the beginning it was not
> so.
>
> And I say unto you, Whosoever shall put away his wife, except
> it be for fornication, and shall marry another, committeth
> adultery: and whoso marrieth her which is put away doth
> commit adultery.                        (Matthew 19:4-9)

Separation is also discouraged in the Bible. Even if the unbelieving partner decides to separate, ideally there should be no remarriage for the Christian according to 1 Corinthians 7:10-11.

What happens when the spiritual bond is undermined by chronic spousal abuse in the marriage? Is there any hope for those who have divorced and remarried? The Bible warns us not be judgmental:

> Who are you to condemn God's servants? They are responsible
> to the Lord, so let him tell them whether they are right or wrong.
> The Lord's power will help them do as they should.
> (Romans 14:4 NLT)

Jesus Christ came, to earth and died, and shed His blood for us. He came to save us from all our sins. And so, according to 1 John, we are assured that:

> If we [freely] admit that we have sinned and confess our sins,
> He is faithful and just (true to His own nature and promises)
> and will forgive our sins [dismiss our lawlessness] and
> [continuously] cleanse us from all unrighteousness [everything
> not in conformity to His will in purpose, thought, and action].
> (1 John 1:9 AMP)

We are warned not to be complacent with God's mercy and faithfulness. We are not to use our freedom as an excuse to do whatever we want, and sin. Paul warned the Galatians:

> For you, brethren, were [indeed] called to freedom; only [do
> not let your] freedom be an incentive to your flesh and an
> opportunity or excuse [for selfishness], but through love you
> should serve one another. (Galatians 5:13 AMP)

## The Effects of Divorce on Kids

Current statistics on the divorce rate in America are alarming and demoralizing. Nearly one of every two marriages could end in divorce, if the current trend continues. It is estimated that more than a million kids are faced with divorce every year. *(Divorce Magazine, www. DivorceMagazine.com and Segue Esprit Inc. Copyright © 1996-2005)*

Divorce can be unnerving and unsettling. With divorce, the spiritual covering over the family becomes compromised. A doorway is opened for demons to enter into the lives of these children. They become angry, depressed, disgruntled, rebellious and have no respect for authority. They stop caring about their studies, and their grades start to fall. Some turn to drugs, sex, alcohol, and other destructive behaviors. The loss of control makes them feel helpless. For these children and their families, the nagging pain of divorce can become worse than death because with death, there is finality, while the pain and torment of divorce linger on. Divorce tends to undermine the sense of commitment to a lifelong marriage and hence children who grow up in a home broken by divorce are more likely to divorce in the future. Contrary to popular opinion, marriage and parenting are not noble and exciting experiments that have failed. Marriage, just like parenting is a divine mandate. It is hard work but rewarding.

Be careful in your courtship, and maintain sexual purity to avoid any unwanted pregnancies. However, if you decide to go ahead with marriage, don't marry out of pity. Know for sure that God will not hold you guiltless, if you break faith with your spouse and get a divorce. Remember this warning from the Bible, "What therefore God has united (joined together), let not man separate or divide" (Mark 10:9 AMP). Children are a blessing and heritage from the Lord. He, therefore, holds you responsible for the way you raise, discipline, and nurture them. God has laid the blueprint in the Bible for how to raise them, so read it and find out all the blessings and its challenges. Even in a bitter divorce court battle, the loss of custody of your children does not exempt you from providing for them.

## The Stepchild Syndrome

Have you ever wondered why stepchildren always have problems, especially, within matrimonial homes? From the beginning of time, every aspect of the human family has come under demonic attack. In the animal kingdom, when a lion, the king of the jungle, takes over a pride, it kills off all the cubs of the dethroned king and starts a family of his own. In humans, our divine nature does not allow us to do that. But the devil incites people to mistreat their stepchildren, and as a result, they are left with insufficient spiritual covering.

Men who do not sire children in a relationship, often tend to show favoritism to their own children, further antagonizing the emotional, psychological, and spiritual stability of the stepchild. Parents should stand in the gap and provide spiritual covering (a spiritual booster) for their children. But if you are spiritually impotent, how are you going to provide any meaningful protection for them?

A two-parent family is stronger than one, so when one parent is not present to raise the kids, part of the spiritual covering for the children is lost.

> Though one may be overpowered, two can defend themselves. A cord of three strands is not quickly broken.
>
> (Ecclesiastes 4:12 NIV)

By yourself, you're unprotected. A person standing alone can be attacked, but two can stand back to back and conquer. Better still, if the Lord of Hosts, Jehovah Tsebaoth (the Lord of the armies), the Lord Jesus Christ (our Rock of ages), is the head of the family, then can the promise come to pass that says:

> One man of you shall put to flight a thousand, for it is the Lord your God Who fights for you, as He promised you.
>
> (Joshua 23:10 AMP)

Don't discriminate against your stepchildren. Work hard to win their approval and love, because God may use them to elevate the family. God looks at the affliction of the disenfranchised, the disillusioned, downtrodden and the orphans to give them relieve from their oppressors. Be careful, God is their avenger.

## The Good News

We serve a merciful and compassionate God, as demonstrated in the parable of the prodigal son. When the son was down and out, he remembered his mistakes and decided to go back to his father.

> And when he came to himself, he said, How many hired
> servants of my father's have bread enough and to spare, and I
> perish with hunger!
>
> I will arise and go to my father, and will say unto him, Father,
> I have sinned against heaven, and before thee, And am no
> more worthy to be called thy son: make me as one of thy hired
> servants. (Luke 15:17-19)

The good news of the above parable was that there was a father waiting. When you become a child of God, He gives you power over evil and the devil.

As Christians, we believe in the existence of a God who is spiritual, but how many people admit to the impact of spiritual reality in a vibrant physical world? How many people have by faith sought the anointing of God in their lives? There are some who don't believe in God or the devil, because Satan, the god of this world, has blinded their minds to the truth, lest they be set free from their spiritual bondage. Paul echoed this sentiment almost two thousand years ago when he said:

> The god of this age has blinded the minds of unbelievers, so that
> they cannot see the light of the gospel of the glory of Christ,
> who is the image of God. (2 Corinthians 4:4 NIV)

Most people are starving spiritually without knowing why. They spend more on their physical needs to the detriment of the spiritual, forgetting that physical life is ephemeral and fleeting, but spiritual things are powerful and permanent according to 2 Corinthians 4:18.

To be honest, things are not going to get any better. Moral decadence will be on the upswing as the age comes to a close. Look around you; the good old days are being replaced with moral decadence in all areas of society, even in the churches as the world heads for destruction. In John we read, "And the world passeth away, and the lust thereof: but he that doeth the will of God abideth forever" (1

John 2:17). There is plenty of evidence that the earth is dying. Seek God and live, say to Him:

> Teach me knowledge and good judgment, for I believe in your commands. Before I was afflicted I went astray, but now I obey your word. You are good, and what you do is good; teach me your decrees. (Psalm 119:66-68 NIV)

We read from the Bible that everybody who calls on the name of the Lord shall be saved as per Joel 2:32, but Paul questions:

> But how can people call for help if they don't know who to trust? And how can they know who to trust if they haven't heard of the One who can be trusted? And how can they hear if nobody tells them? And how is anyone going to tell them, unless someone is sent to do it? That's why Scripture exclaims, A sight to take your breath away! Grand processions of people telling all the good things of God! But not everybody is ready for this, ready to see and hear and act. Isaiah asked what we all ask at one time or another: "Does anyone care, God? Is anyone listening and believing a word of it?"
> (Romans 10:14-16 MSG)

In our troubled relationship and in our brokenness, only God can help us to spiritually reconnect, reconcile, and redirect our energies for our mutual benefit and edification.

# Chapter Seven

## Rebuilding Relationships

*The hand of the LORD was upon me, and he brought me out by the Spirit of the LORD and set me in the middle of a valley; it was full of bones. He led me back and forth among them, and I saw a great many bones on the floor of the valley, bones that were very dry. He asked me, "Son of man, can these bones live?" I said, "O Sovereign LORD, you alone know." Then he said to me, "Prophesy to these bones and say to them, 'Dry bones, hear the word of the LORD! This is what the Sovereign LORD says to these bones: I will make breath enter you, and you will come to life. I will attach tendons to you and make flesh come upon you and cover you with skin; I will put breath in you, and you will come to life. Then you will know that I am the LORD.' "*         *(Ezekiel 37:1-6 NIV)*

In Western scientific culture, spiritual healing is often trivialized or marginalized. But if human beings are both spiritual and physical, why not prescribe therapies that deal with the spiritual in tandem with the physical? Why not invoke the belief system of the individual when appropriate and make it truly holistic? Why is it only when a person is dying, when all else has failed, that we start looking to the spiritual? Then again, if death is spiritual, and is the finality of the physical, why not spiritually treat the physical before it dies?

Today, too many people are experiencing marital problems, with many marriages ending in divorce because of lack of spiritual knowledge. Here are two reasons why. The first deals with spiritual seeds, and the second, with the marital soil. The Bible tells us that a man reaps what he sows. This brings three main things to mind, the seed, the soil, and the harvest.

Going back to the analogy of the marriage garden, I find first of all, that some have not planted any spiritual seeds in the marital garden, and so come harvest time they have nothing. They are also not prepared, should famine or difficult times come. But ignorance is no excuse.

There are those who may have planted some seeds, but it all depends on the kinds of seeds and the quantity of seed sown. There are six things God hates, and a one more that He detests with passion in a relationship: "eyes that are arrogant (*the spirit that makes one overestimate himself and underestimate others*), a tongue that lies, hands that murder the innocent, a heart that hatches evil plots, feet that race down a wicked track, a mouth that lies under oath, a troublemaker in the family" (Proverbs 6:16-19 MSG. *Comments added*). For those who may have planted non-spiritual seeds; such as selfishness, apathy or domineering tendencies; these yield nothing but bushes and thorns to choke the marriage from bearing any fruits. In the end, there is no true growth in the marriage. The Bible warns that whoever sows to the wind will reap the whirlwind, and he who sows iniquity, will reap vanity (Hosea 8:7).

Only those who planted spiritual seeds, such as love, joy, peace, patience, kindness, goodness, faithfulness, gentleness, and self-control under the auspices of the Holy Spirit will bear lasting fruits, and bring life into the marriage. Here is a helpful spiritual insight: "Whoever sows sparingly will also reap sparingly, and whoever sows generously will also reap generously." (2 Corinthians 9:6 NIV)

The second reason why marriages do not succeed depends on the marital soil in which the seeds were planted. The Bible again says:

> For he who sows to his own flesh (lower nature, sensuality) will from the flesh reap decay and ruin and destruction, but he who sows to the Spirit will from the Spirit reap eternal life.
> (Galatians 6:8 AMP)

Some have tilled, and watered the garden but to no avail. Lasting spiritual fruits are illusion because these marriages are often founded on the shifting sands of worldly philosophies, such as humanism, science, technology, and pop-psychology. The derivatives of these so-called good lives, are nothing but vanity, and depend on materialistic, and hedonistic tendencies to prop up the marriage. On the other hand, good and lasting spiritual fruits can only grow on godly watered soil, of which the foundation is none other than Christ Jesus, the solid, spiritual bedrock. The teachings of Jesus give life, and so He says:

> He who believes in Me [who cleaves to and trusts in and relies on Me] as the Scripture has said, from his innermost being shall flow [continuously] springs and rivers of living water.
> (John 7:38 AMP)

> The [Holy] Spirit and the bride (the church, the true Christians) say, Come! And let him who is listening say, Come! And let everyone come who is thirsty [who is painfully conscious of his need of those things by which the soul is refreshed, supported, and strengthened]; and whoever [earnestly] desires to do it, let him come, take, appropriate, and drink the water of Life without cost.
> (Revelation 22:17 AMP)

Here is a caveat; every marriage goes through some unexplained hardships, or dryness. There will come a time of famine, or turmoil to put a strain on the marriage. King Solomon, a man who perhaps knows more about love and marriage, a man who married seven hundred women, besides three hundred concubines wrote, "Then you must protect me from the foxes, foxes on the prowl, Foxes who would like nothing better than to get into our flowering garden" (Song of Solomon 2:15 MSG). The devil will come and attempt to steal, kill, and destroy the fruits of the marriage. In times like these, we all need divine intervention. My advice is to seek spiritual knowledge. God knows why He said in Hosea 4:6 that His people perish for lack of (spiritual) knowledge. Listen to the Creator of holy matrimony, and take a cue from the Valley of dry bones. If your marriage has been spiritually vandalized, or dried up, or is sick and on life support, prophesy life back into your marriage. Seek the spring of living waters and your marriage would be "...like a tree firmly planted [and tended] by the streams of water, ready to bring forth its fruit in its season; its leaf also shall not fade or wither" (Psalm 1:3 AMP). Look to Jesus, and seek the empowerment of the Holy Spirit. Your marriage will prosper and come to maturity.

## The What, How, Why, and Who

When there is a problem or something goes wrong, people tend to analyze the situation by what happened, how it started, who caused it, and why. However, when it comes to healing and restoration, the scientific mind set primarily looks at the what and the how of the problem. When they look at the why, it is still within the context of the what and the how. Investigating the why of the problem eventually leads to the who. However, to the unspiritual, the who becomes a person and has nothing to do with God or the devil. To them, "Out of sight is out of mind," and "Seeing is believing" are their mottos. Anything outside their five senses is incomprehensible. This kind of thinking always falls short of finding a lasting solution to relational problems. What they fail to realize is that before something bad happens in the physical, its source can be traced to the spiritual. My favorite example is the story of David and Bathsheba. David saw Bathsheba, a beautiful woman, bathing. He lusted after her beauty and inquired about her. He was told that she was a married woman but David used his position as king to commit adultery with Bathsheba. When she became pregnant, he engineered the death of Uriah, her husband. God was displeased with David.

For his punishment, God told David through the prophet Nathan:

> I anointed you king over Israel, and I delivered you from the hand of Saul. I gave your master's house to you, and your

master's wives into your arms. I gave you the house of Israel and Judah. And if all this had been too little, I would have given you even more.

Why did you despise the word of the LORD by doing what is evil in his eyes? You struck down Uriah the Hittite with the sword and took his wife to be your own. You killed him with the sword of the Ammonites.

Now, therefore, the sword will never depart from your house, because you despised me and took the wife of Uriah the Hittite to be your own.

This is what the LORD says: "Out of your own household I am going to bring calamity upon you. Before your very eyes I will take your wives and give them to one who is close to you, and he will lie with your wives in broad daylight. You did it in secret, but I will do this thing in broad daylight before all Israel."

Then David said to Nathan, "I have sinned against the LORD." Nathan replied, "The LORD has taken away your sin. You are not going to die. But because by doing this you have made the enemies of the LORD show utter contempt, the son born to you will die."                    (2 Samuel 12:7-14 NIV)

The baby born to David died. Later, Ammon, one of David's sons, allowed infatuation and lust to blind his better judgment, and he raped his stepsister, Tamar, Absalom's sister. The spirit of hatred later entered into Ammon and Ammon hated her with intense hatred. In fact, his hatred for his sister was more than the professed love (lust) he had for her. Out of revenge, Absalom killed Ammon. In the course of time, the spirit of covetousness entered into Absalom, who was very handsome, and loved by David, to covet after David's throne. He succeeded in running David out of town. He then set up a tent on a roof and, on the advice of Ahithophel, had sex with his father's concubines in broad daylight, hence fulfilling the prophecy of the LORD.

When you know the spiritual why, you are able to flee all sexual immoralities, because God is a Holy God and He wants us to be holy. Without holiness, we become unclean and defiled, and we cannot fellowship with Him. Sexual immorality and sexual impurities hurt your body as you keep attaching and detaching yourself spiritually with other people, other than your original soul mate or partner. How do you keep yourself pure? This calls for spiritual wisdom and instructions. Always start by spiritualizing!

## Always Spiritualize

If you attend church, and listen to sermon after sermon, but do not apply what you hear to your life, you gain nothing. You are merely being religious. Your religiosity becomes an act, something you put on out of sentimentality, to please yourself, and to win the praise of men instead of God. True Spirituality, on the other hand, is the application of inner principles based on one's faith to glorify God and the edification (spiritual improvement) of mankind.

Spirituality is akin to applied scientific principles. In science, everything has a cause and an effect. Events and conditions are not random. There is order. The scientist, therefore, looks for patterns to establish a connection in order to arrive at a conclusion. In this regard, we need to be scientific with the way we practice our spirituality. How many people believe that spirituality has a lot to do with the bad choices people make in life, causing unnecessary turmoil and suffering in their relationships?

We live in a world in which the spiritual is superimposed on the physical, with the physical dovetailing into the spiritual. As such, nothing in this world happens by chance. Therefore, the spiritual mind-set looks at the physical through the eyes of the spiritual. People who allow events in their lives to pass, without connecting them to spiritual issues, do not only understand what is happening to them, they cannot do anything to change their circumstances or world.

Spiritualizing does not mean you renege on the physical. In your relationships, be careful not to get into legalized spirituality, which can easily lead to spiritual pride. Instead, through love, show justice tempered with mercy.

The unspiritual and the spiritual both agree that people should stop giving excuses and take responsibility for their actions. There is agreement on the what and the how of a situation, but the divergence comes in the why and the who in finding a lasting solution. The unspiritual does not believe that there are spiritual forces behind every social vice, and problems in our lives. The devil can influence your choice of where you seek help, directing you to evil, or contrary agents to worsen your situation. Beware of the so-called marriage counselors and experts, and pop psychologist who pay lip service to the Word of God to teach human philosophy to worsen your situation through bad counseling. Or else, when the demons return with seven spirits, more wicked than themselves, the battle to regain control of your situation will be seven times harder.

The spiritual man acknowledges the existence of a higher divine authority, and believes that human beings, as well as the rest of the universe, are the handiwork of a Creator, and not an act of some random phenomenon, as evolutionists would have us believe. There are those such as the New Agers, who have replaced the spiritual who, with a force--the subconscious mind. However, when people do things unconsciously it can be dangerous and injurious to their relationships.

In Eastern mysticism, people are taught to blank out their mind and let the subconscious take over. Don't become a victim of your subconsciousness. Don't you know that the mind is a spiritual battleground, between the forces of good and evil? Don't yield your mind to the demons of mind-control, to destroy your relationship. Be careful, the devil doesn't shoot blanks, and so if you don't learn to forgive, and forget, the devil will remind you of all the hurts that you cannot let go to demoralize you, and hurt your partner, as you trade vicious verbal jabs during power struggles. If your marriage is in trouble, seek spiritual help. Seek biblical counseling.

One major advantage of counseling is that it frees you from bondage to your subconsciousness by prompting you to communicate your feelings verbally. Your partner is not a mind reader. Although good communicational and interpersonal skills are important, the spiritual dimension provides much more. Be careful of your vocabulary and diction because there is death and life in the power of the tongue according to Proverbs 18:21. The words we speak have power either to bless or curse, to encourage and build up or to break down, devastate, and destroy someone. A person can open his or her mouth and pronounce a curse and it will come to pass. A spiritual entity, whether good or evil, acts on those words to bring to pass what has been uttered. Jesus told His disciples:

> The Spirit gives life; the flesh counts for nothing. The words I have spoken to you are spirit and they are life. For by your words you will be acquitted, and by your words you will be condemned. (John 6:63; Matthew 12:37 NIV)

Since the root cause of many relational problems are spiritually induced, why not always think spiritual before speaking? Let the agape love for your partner dictate your thinking, and behavior. Words can kill and give life; they're either poison or fruit--the choice is yours. Remove *separation* and *divorce* from you marital vocabulary. In earlier times, Moses warned the ancient Israelites:

> Take to heart all the words I have solemnly declared to you this day, so that you may command your children to obey carefully all the words of this law. They are not just idle words for you-- they are your life. (Deuteronomy 32:46-47 NIV)

God is spiritual. His commandments are therefore spiritually based to transform our lives. Remember, there is interaction between the physical and spiritual realms and so when God decrees something it comes to pass. Any violations of His laws have consequences. But our God is a loving God, who tempers justice with mercy. He knows all our weaknesses and is very patient with us. In fact, He has already prepared an antidote to free us from our sinful nature from death to life, even before the foundation of the world through His Son Jesus. Read the Bible and find out about this antidote, and avail yourself of His saving grace.

The key to solving our problems lies in the realm of the spirit and not in mere men. Man is just the agent. Those who depend solely on men, and worldly philosophies are doomed. People who rely on so-called marriage experts, and violate God's commandments are being misled. In Jeremiah we read:

> This is what the LORD says: "Cursed is the one who trusts in man, who depends on flesh for his strength and whose heart turns away from the LORD. (Jeremiah 17:5 NIV)

God intended for humans to marry; male to female, and to multiply and subdue the earth. As long as the earth is in place, this decree is immutable, together with the rules and guidelines associated with this mandate. However, there are evil forces bent on interfering with God's mandates for the family structure and the marriage institution. To those who think they are wiser than God, or think His decrees are outmoded, hear this:

> What if some did not believe and were without faith? Does their lack of faith and their faithlessness nullify and make ineffective and void the faithfulness of God and His fidelity [to His Word]? By no means! Let God be found true though every human being is false and a liar, as it is written, That You may be justified and shown to be upright in what You say, and prevail when You are judged [by sinful men].
> (Romans 3:3-4 AMP)

The spiritual does not change. It is the physical that changes. The nature of God does not change, and so Jesus said; *"Heaven and earth will pass away, but my words will never pass away" (Matthew 24:35)*. This present world is under the dominion of Satan and his demonic powers. His propaganda machine has been working overtime to shape the minds and attitudes of people contrary to the things of God since the days of Paradise, when he beguiled the woman, and said:

> You will not surely die, the serpent said to the woman. "For God knows that when you eat of it your eyes will be opened, and you will be like God, knowing good and evil."

> When the woman saw that the fruit of the tree was good for food
> and pleasing to the eye, and also desirable for gaining wisdom,
> she took some and ate it. She also gave some to her husband,
> who was with her, and he ate it.                    (Genesis 3:4-6 NIV)

Evil spirits still operate in the children of disobedience. Their aim is to destroy our relationship with one another, and also with God. How can we fight an unseen enemy? The battle is the Lord's and so He has made available to us, all the spiritual arsenal we need to win this battle through our Lord Jesus Christ. As children of the Most High God, we are assured of victory as follows:

> You, dear children, are from God and have overcome them,
> because the one who is in you is greater than the one who is in
> the world. They are from the world and therefore speak from
> the viewpoint of the world, and the world listens to them.
>
> We are from God, and whoever knows God listens to us; but
> whoever is not from God does not listen to us. This is how we
> recognize the Spirit of truth and the spirit of falsehood.
>                                             (1 John 4:4-6 NIV)

God has entrusted human beings, the higher species created in His image, as the custodians of this earth. As such, He holds each person accountable for how he or she contributes to the quality of life on this planet. But God has not left us helpless, or clueless. Seek knowledge and instruction, because for the lack of knowledge we perish. In the Gospels Jesus assures us:

> For verily I say unto you, That whosoever shall say unto this
> mountain, Be thou removed, and be thou cast into the sea; and
> shall not doubt in his heart, but shall believe that those things
> which he saith shall come to pass; he shall have whatsoever he
> saith.                                          (Mark 11:23)

The spiritual principle here is that, if there are marital mountains in your family, ask God to give you what it takes to amend, and sustain your marriage and you shall have whatsoever you request. If your relationships with people are in trouble, or are as dry bones, brittle and are about to break, stand on the Word of God which is Spirit and life. Prophesy, decree and declare: love, peace, joy happiness, blessings, mutual respect, truthfulness, faithfulness forgiveness, mercy, tender loving care (TLC), wisdom, humility, togetherness, self-control, favor, prosperity, health, and life into your broken relationships. The above list constitutes some of the things the devil steals from you. Don't be surprised if you have tried to change your spouse and it hasn't worked, don't worry, only the Holy Spirit can truly change, or transform a person, and so in Zachariah 4:6 we read, [It is] not by might, nor by power, but my Spirit says the Lord Almighty."

Our earthly troubles are the results of our spiritual battles. That is why we should always base our spirituality on the Word of God as found in the Bible. When we spiritualize, we in effect invoke divine assistance by acknowledging that God exists, and that He hears us. By seeking spiritual counsel, we avoid the ignorance or lack of spiritual knowledge, that demonic spirits have used to their advantage to hurt us.

The spiritual man, led by the Holy Spirit, is alert to the nature of the spiritual warfare in his life and is protected. Don't get blindsided or victimized in your marriage and other family relationships. Be wise, acquire spiritual knowledge and instructions, and fortify yourself.

In spiritual warfare, we stand on the legal authority of God, delegated to us through our Lord Jesus Christ, to wrestle from the devil all that he has stolen from us. According to John 10:10, the devil only comes to steal, kill, and destroy what belongs to us, but Jesus came to save and liberate us from this spiritual foe.

The devil and the influences of evil are real. Those who ignore this fact are vulnerable to spiritual attacks. In fact the devil has already possessed their spiritual gates and taken them prisoners and as slaves. But our God Jehovah is a mighty Warrior. He will fight for you if you call on Him. Remember, our fight is not against flesh and blood.

# Don't Victimize Your Spouse

When you realize you're not fighting against flesh and blood, you will understand why Jesus gave the commandment to "love your neighbor as yourself" (Mark 12:33 NIV). Satan starts a conflict, and tries to play both camps. When a Christian assaults a victim of Satan, the devil wins twice. The key is to attack your problems, not your spouse.

There are those that the devil uses to do his dirty work. As soon as the attack or punishment comes, he leaves them to face the consequences by themselves. More sorrowful and pitiful are the witches and wizards who become pawns and stooges of the devil to harass, steal, torment, destroy, and kill their own family members. However, these poor souls are themselves victims, so forgive them.

> To whom ye forgive any thing, I forgive also: for if I forgave any thing, to whom I forgave it, for your sakes forgave I it in the person of Christ; Lest Satan should get an advantage of us: for we are not ignorant of his devices. (2 Corinthians 2:10-11)

Christians tend to shoot and bury their wounded. Anybody who does not forgive his brother or sister plays into the devil's hands. Don't destroy your spouse to win your case. It is better to win the peace than your case.

If you are experiencing bitterness in your marriage or other relationships and do not know what to do, cry unto Jesus just as Moses did. In Exodus 15:22-25, he cried unto God in the wilderness when the ancient Israelites encountered the bitter waters of Marah. God showed Moses a piece of wood, and he threw it into the water and it became sweet. The cross of Jesus is that piece of wood. Hand over all your burdens to Jesus on the cross. The words of Jesus are spirit, and life to revive, reinvigorate, and resurrect your marriage.

God has set in place spiritual truths, guidelines and principles, laws and regulations, to maintain relations between men and women. He has made it plain how we are to live and what we are to do. We are to be fair and just to our neighbor, and compassionate and loyal in love.

> He has showed you, O man, what is good. And what does the Lord require of you but to do justly, and to love kindness and mercy, and to humble yourself and walk humbly with your God? (Micah 6:8 AMP)

First, pray for the ability to love and the capacity to express that love in your life. Remember, not all disagreements are bad. Sometimes these are wake-up calls to alert you to potential problems in your life or relationships. Be patient and seek divine guidance. For a Christian, problems in your life should push you closer to God. By faith, you are to trust and totally depend on Him, to see you through and to accomplish His purpose for your life.

In the meanwhile, learn to resolve problems without bitterness, and dissension. Then sweeten your marriage with humility, truth, respect and a heavy dose of TLC (Tender Loving Care). The key to maintaining peace in any relationship hinges on our love and devotion to God and our love for our fellow human beings.

## Love Covers a Multitude of Sins

Hatred stirs up dissension, but divine love covers over all wrongs because love:

> It does not rejoice at injustice and unrighteousness, but rejoices when right and truth prevail.

> Love bears up under anything and everything that comes, is ever ready to believe the best of every person, its hopes are fadeless under all circumstances, and it endures everything [without weakening].

> Love never fails [never fades out or becomes obsolete or comes to an end]. As for prophecy (the gift of interpreting the divine will and purpose), it will be fulfilled and pass away; as for tongues, they will be destroyed and cease; as for knowledge, it will pass away [it will lose its value and be superseded by truth].

> When I was a child, I talked like a child, I thought like a child, I reasoned like a child; now that I have become a man, I am done with childish ways and have put them aside.

> And so faith, hope, love abide [faith--conviction and belief respecting man's relation to God and divine things; hope--joyful and confident expectation of eternal salvation; love--true affection for God and man, growing out of God's love for and in us], these three; but the greatest of these is love.
> (1 Corinthians 13:6-8, 11, 13 AMP)

Satan is an instigator and a reactionary. He starts fights to frustrate, harass the saints, and obstruct God's kingdom in every way he can. It's good spiritual warfare strategy to counterattack by taking action in the opposite way from evil. For example, avoid being a litigant, and do not become too legalistic in your relationships. In other words, rise above the law and aim for perfection. These spiritual principles are embodied in the advice Jesus gave us when he said:

> Ye have heard that it hath been said, Thou shalt love thy neighbour, and hate thine enemy.

> But I say unto you, Love your enemies, bless them that curse you, do good to them that hate you, and pray for them which despitefully use you, and persecute you;

> That ye may be the children of your Father, which is in heaven: for he maketh his sun to rise on the evil and on the good, and sendeth rain on the just and on the unjust.

> For if ye love them, which love you, what reward have ye? Do not even the publicans the same?

> And if ye salute your brethren only, what do ye more than others? Do not even the publicans so?

> Be ye therefore perfect, even as your Father, which is in heaven, is perfect.
> (Matthew 5:43-48)

Where there is hate, start loving. Where you feel anger, act to bring calm. Where there is greed, start giving. It is not only more blessed to give than to receive, it is also contagious. Where there are large egos, be a servant to all. Humility will always defeat pride and deflate all egos and bring you honor. To the spiritually mature, Jesus advised that whoever wants to be the greatest must be the servant of all. Where there is backbiting and gossip, say things to build people up. Under the inspiration of the Holy Spirit, Paul counseled:

> Finally, brothers, whatever is true, whatever is noble, whatever is right, whatever is pure, whatever is lovely, whatever is admirable--if anything is excellent or praiseworthy--think about [*and say*] such things.
> (Philippians 4:8 NIV. *Comments added*)

We can only accomplish praiseworthy things when we trust in God and set our mind on the things of God, because He keeps in perfect peace the one whose mind is focused on Him (Isaiah 26:3).

As a child of God, you have been called to a life of perfection; and therefore, the Spirit in you thrives for excellence. Focus on the positives, and where there is disunity, try and find a way to bring people together. For even "When a man's ways are pleasing to the LORD, he makes even his enemies live at peace with him" according (Proverbs 16:7 NIV).

When you understand the spiritual why, it will lead you to see the end from the beginning, God's plan and purpose for your life as you endure the triumphant results of your trials as stated in Romans 8:18. You will not conform any longer to the pattern of this world, but be transformed by the renewing of your mind, to prove for yourself what God's will is--His good, pleasing, and perfect will for your life (Romans 12:2). You'll be changed from the inside out when you fix your attention on God. He will bring the best out of you.

> And God is able to make all grace abound to you, so that in all things at all times, having all that you need, you will abound in every good work. As it is written: "He has scattered abroad his gifts to the poor; his righteousness endures forever." Now he who supplies seed to the sower and bread for food will also supply and increase your store of seed and will enlarge the harvest of your righteousness.
> (2 Corinthians 9:8-10)

People become stingy in an attempt to have more, but what they don't realize is that it is when you let go of what is in your hands that God gives you more. As written, "One man gives freely, yet gains even more; another withholds unduly, but comes to poverty" (Proverbs 11:24 NIV). Whatever personal gifts you have, were given to you by God to serve others. You increase as you use your time, talent (expertise), and treasure (money) to serve others. The unspiritual, however does not understand or subscribe to the above spiritual wisdom. They tend to exploit their position and use their authority to further their own selfish agendas. As a man thinks, so he is! In the end, the devil fuels their self-aggrandizement tendencies to make them believe that whatever they have been able to achieve comes from their own efforts, hence robbing God of His glory.

When you know the why and the who rather than the what, you are able to show compassion, because you understand why Jesus had compassion on the multitudes. The aim of the enemy is to harass people spiritually (Matthew 9:36) and wear down the saints (Daniel 7:25). A true Christian is a peacemaker. The world would be a better place if people would accentuate on the positives, and love their neighbors as commanded by God. Jesus, in Matthew 5:9, said "Blessed are the peacemakers: for they shall be called the children of God."

When you understand the why, you will be able to bless those who despitefully use you (Matthew 5:44) because you will realize they are also victims (collateral damage), in the ongoing spiritual warfare.

## To Forgive, or Not to Forgive?

When you foresee the spiritual why, you will be able to forgive people of their trespasses and not let the sun go down on your anger, thereby giving the devil a legal foothold to mess around with your relationships (Ephesians 4:26). The Bible exhorts us as follows:

> Therefore, as God's chosen people, holy and dearly loved, clothe yourselves with compassion, kindness, humility, gentleness and patience. Bear with each other and forgive whatever grievances

you may have against one another. Forgive as the Lord forgave
you. And over all these virtues put on love, which binds them
all together in perfect unity.        (Colossians 3:12-14 NIV)

According to Richard Ing, pastor and author of *Spiritual Warfare,*
one of the most insidious of curses is unforgiveness. Unforgiveness
is a hated sin in God's eyes and a strong legal ground for Satan to
attack you. If you do not forgive others of their sins against you,
neither will God forgive your sins against Him (Matthew 6:15).
Thus the curses derived from your sins continue to work in your life,
as long as you hold a grudge and don't forgive your neighbor.

In Matthew, Jesus told a parable of a servant whose master forgave
him of a huge debt. But as soon as this servant left his master's
presence, he met one of his fellow servants who owed him pennies
compared to what was owed the master. He demanded payment of
the debt owed him. When his fellow servant could not pay him but
pleaded for leniency, the first servant cast him into prison.

> Then his lord, after that he had called him, said unto him. O
> though wicked servant, I forgave thee all that debt, because
> thou desiredst me: shouldest not thou also have had compassion
> on thy fellow servant, even as I had pity on thee? And his lord
> was wroth, and delivered him to the tormentors, till he should
> pay all that was due unto him.        (Matthew 18:32-34)

Jesus then said, "So likewise shall my heavenly Father do also unto
you, if ye from your hearts forgive not every one his brother their
trespasses" (vs. 35). One of the meanings of the word *tormentors*
is "demons." Jesus taught us to forgive others because God will not
accept your sacrifices, if you have anything against your brother, *or
spouse* according to Matthew 5:22-25.

You and your spouse have needs and expectations that are fulfilled
by the resources you both bring to the marriage. Whatever both of
you saw in each other before the union should be cherished, and
nurtured. Paul exhorts us to:

> Be gentle and forbearing with one another and, if one has a
> difference (a grievance or complaint) against another, readily
> pardoning each other; even as the Lord has [freely] forgiven
> you, so must you also [forgive].        (Colossians 3:13 AMP)

He who forgives others will be forgiven, and in Matthew 5:7 we read
the merciful shall receive mercy. For the Christian, no matter the
hurt, you don't say, *"I can never forgive you, or I can forgive but not
forget."* You cannot but Jesus can! Why do you suppose it is written
in Philippians chapter 4:13, "I can do all things through Christ who
strengthens me." Does Jesus lives in you? If your answer is yes, then
reach down inside you and allow the Christ who lives in you to do
the forgiving. Allow Jesus to do His work of carrying your pains, the
hurt, the heartache, the bitterness, your cares, and all your anxieties
on the cross for you, because He loves you. When that happens, the
Christ who leaves in you will reach out to the image of God in your
fellow man. At first Presbyterian Church of Irvington, New Jersey,
this principle is at the root of our congregational greetings after Holy
Communion, where we turn to one another and say, "The Christ in
me greets the Christ in you."

The spiritual battle over your life right now is between good and
evil, between God and the devil. You are either on God's side or
the devil's. There is no middle ground. So choose wisely. Don't be
deceived by the New Age movement that is sweeping the Western
world. Eastern mysticism is currently gaining widespread influence
because it has couched its teachings in scientific and medical
terminologies to deceive the unspiritual. Don't be deceived by those
who say, "No true vision or visionary takes sides (in any religion),"
because God's law is imprinted on our hearts. Pushed to its logical
conclusion, all religions contain some God-given truths and therefore
lead to the same God.

Some people maintain that we don't need intermediaries to get to
God. But it is only through self-realization, and through one's inner
spirit, that the soul or spirit can evolve and achieve oneness with
God. This is half-truth, and half lies, and therefore a false religion,
or gospel. The underlying philosophy here is that everything in the

universe is part of the divine consciousness, whatever that is, and there are no distinctions between the created and the Creator. These New Agers claim you are only subjected to the choices you make, whether good or bad, and have nothing to do with God, or the devil. Armed with this false knowledge and partial truths, many people have become their own intermediaries, to do whatever is pleasing in their eyes.

In effect, they are saying, "Who is Jehovah God, and who is Jesus Christ, and who are those who claim to be His priests and pastors that I should listen and obey them?" Jesus said, "Seek the truth and the truth shall set you free" (John 8:32). What then is there to do spiritually, to protect your marriage and family?

The key is to pursue divine love, flee all sexual immoralities and impurities, and stay in a monogamous relation with your spouse. Sexual sins are pleasurable, but they could kill you, physically and spiritually. For example, by engaging in casual or oral sex, you can unknowingly attract herpes or HIV, which can then be passed on to your children in a situation where they happen to drink behind you from the same cup.

Spiritual marriage may be non-sexual but always about control. Don't be the one in your family who becomes the conduit for demons and evil spirits to invade your spiritual space and to gain access to your family, subjecting them to all kinds of spiritual and physical enslavements, such as poverty, greed, theft, incarceration, fornication, divorce, infertility, abortion, sexual immoralities, homosexuality, alcoholism, rage, spousal abuse, pride, low self-esteem, depression, suicide, and premature birth or death. Arm yourself with biblical truths and spiritual principles. Study and learn how to use the Word of God so as to glorify Him in your life. In Hosea, God laments our lack of spiritual knowledge.

> My people are destroyed for lack of knowledge: because thou hast rejected knowledge, I will also reject thee, that thou shalt be no priest to me: seeing thou hast forgotten the law of thy God, I will also forget thy children.          (Hosea 4:6)

> For the priest's lips should guard and keep pure the knowledge
> [of My law], and the people should seek (inquire for and require)
> instruction at his mouth; for he is the messenger of the Lord of
> hosts.                                                     (Malachi 2:7 AMP)

It is our responsibility to acquire spiritual knowledge and instruction to defend our homes, our loved ones, and ourselves against all spiritual intrusions to our relationships. What you don't know is out there spiritually may be hunting your family, like a game, with the breakdown of your marriage, and family relationships, as trophies.

In spiritual warfare, people get hurt and relationships are shattered or destroyed. Don't lose hope or be discouraged. Let the Holy Spirit do His work of being your Comforter, the one who helps and empowers you to disregard the verbal jabs or demon talk, in order to focus on Jesus. Without the Holy Spirit, wherein lies your power to fight evil? The Holy Spirit is the one who teaches you how to war and your fingers to fight (Psalm 144:1). We read in Zechariah 4:6, it is "Not by might, nor by power, but by my spirit, saith the LORD of hosts." He is your Advocate! He intercedes on your behalf with groans, which words cannot express (Romans 8:26). Allow Him to work wonders in your life, and relationships.

Satan and his demonic hordes are relentless. That is why Paul, in 1 Thessalonians 5:17, exhorts us to pray without ceasing. In order to win our spiritual battles, we must be vigilant and well prepared at all times to fight (with fasting and spiritual-warfare prayers). But remember this, the battle is the Lord's. He is the Lord of Hosts; He will fight for you and so He says:

> Have not I commanded thee? Be strong and of a good courage;
> be not afraid, neither be thou dismayed: for the LORD thy God
> is with thee whithersoever thou goest.                    (Joshua 1:9)

> For the LORD your God is he that goeth with you, to fight for
> you against your enemies, to save you.    (Deuteronomy 20:4)

# AMEN

# Appendix
# Power Prayers

# Power Prayers For Marriage & Family Restoration

Adapted from *Target or weapon: The Prayer Book*
By Ebenezer Gyasi

## *Tearing Down Barriers*

*We are human, but we don't wage war with human plans and methods.*

*We use God's mighty weapons, not mere worldly weapons, to knock down the Devil's strongholds.*

*With these weapons we break down every proud argument that keeps people from knowing God. With these weapons we conquer their rebellious ideas, and we teach them to obey Christ.*

*And we will punish those who remained disobedient after the rest of you became loyal and obedient.        (2 Corinthians 10:3-6 NLT)*

# By Ebenezer Gyasi
Deliverance-On-The Go Ministries
P.O. Box 3565
Newark, NJ 07103

# Marriage

## Demons that have been assigned to fight against my Marriage hear me, and obey!

## Spiritual Marriages

Heavenly Father, Creator of heaven and earth, Jehovah-Elohim, Jehovah Nissi, Jehovah Shalom, Jehovah-M'kaddesh, institutor of marriage and family. In the most powerful name of our Lord Jesus Christ, my God, my Lord and Master, my Deliverer and Protector, I ask for the anointing to destroy, and sever any evil spiritual unions fighting against my family. I bind all demons of spiritual marriages in my life.

Heavenly Father, You did not institute holy matrimony between humans and demons. You ordained marriage as a union between men and women. Father, You said in Genesis, "For this reason a man will leave his father and mother and be united to his wife, and they will become one flesh" (Genesis 2:24).

Father, I stand on Your word, and I break every spiritual marriage to any demonic spirits. I use the blood of Jesus to sever any soul, or marital ties to ancestral, river, marine, serpentine, and all other demonic spirits.

Any demonic spirit married to me spiritually or physically, I divorce you in the deliverance name of Jesus Christ of Nazareth.
I command you to leave me now and never come back. I belong to Jesus; you no longer have control over me. If for some reason you decide to attack me, may the Holy Spirit fire torment, and consume you, in the name of Jesus, I command. Amen.

Heavenly Father, Jehovah-Nissi, El-Shaddai, Jehovah Jireh, Jehovah Shalom, I give You the glory. Father, in the most powerful and deliverance name of our Lord Jesus Christ, my Lord and Master, my Deliverer and Protector, I rebuke and bind all demons that have sold my marriage on the spiritual market.

No matter whom it has been sold to or where it is, I recover my marriage, and the joy of marriage by fire in the name of Jesus and by the power of the Holy Spirit. Lord Jesus, sanctify my marriage by thy blood unto Your holy, mighty name. Amen

## Heart, Soul and Mind Ties

In the precious name of our Lord Jesus Christ, my God, my Lord and Master, my Savior and Protector, Heavenly Father, Jehovah-Nissi, Jehovah Tsidqenu, Jehovah Shalom, I loose my heart, soul, and mind in the demonic realm. I sever all heart, soul and mind ties with dead relatives.

I sever all ties with demonic spirits associated with any cult heroes, dead or alive, who may have captured my imagination, and have become a snare to me.

I sever all ties with those who are holding my marriage captive and would not let me experience peace, love, true joy, and fulfillment in my marriage.

I rebuke them. I bind them. I cast them out in the mighty name of Jesus Christ of Nazareth. I fill their place with love, peace and joy by the power of the Holy Spirit, to the glory of God, in the name of Jesus I command, Amen.

## Dream Attackers

Heavenly Father, Jehovah-Nissi, Jehovah Shalom, in the mighty name of our Lord Jesus Christ, I come against all powers of darkness that visit or attack me in my dreams. I rebuke, bind, and destroy all demons and spirits that romance, and have sex with me in my dreams. I rebuke demons of sexual perversion (name them).

Demons, listen to me. I soak my sex life with the blood of Jesus, and so you have no right to sleep with me. In the name of Jesus, I command you to leave me right now, and never come back. May the fire of the Holy Spirit consume you, if you ever come near me. In the protective name of Jesus, I pray. Amen.

## Demons of Barrenness

Heavenly Father, Jehovah-Nissi, Jehovah Shalom, in the precious name of our Lord Jesus Christ, my God, my Lord and Master, my Deliverer and Protector, and by the power of the Holy Spirit, I soak myself in the blood of Jesus.

I rebuke, I bind, and break the powers of all demons that have been tinkering with my reproductive organs and have vowed never to allow me to have children. I break all curses that have been placed on my reproductive organs.

By the blood of Jesus, I release the virility and potency of my sexuality. In the most powerful name of Jesus Christ of Nazareth, I will be fruitful and bear children because children are a blessing and a heritage of the Lord. Hallelujah! Amen!

In the powerful name of our Lord Jesus Christ, my God, my Lord and

Master, my Deliverer and Protector, Heavenly Father, Jehovah-Nissi, Jehovah-M'kaddesh, Jehovah Shalom, I stand on Your Word, which says if I worship the Lord my God, Your blessings will be on my food, and water, and that You will take away sickness from me, and I will not miscarry or be barren in the land (Exodus 23:25-26).

I therefore rebuke, and bind all demons of barrenness that are fighting against me. Every spiritual abortionist, every spirit of Herod hunting the seed of my womb (or body), I bind and destroy your powers in the name of Jesus. Amen.

## Trouble Causing Demons

In the most loving and powerful name of our Lord Jesus Christ, my God, my Lord and Master, my Deliverer and Protector, Heavenly Father, Jehovah-Nissi, Jehovah Shalom, according to Your Word in Proverbs 6:16-19, there are six things You hate, and one more that You loathe with a passion: eyes that are arrogant, a tongue that lies, hands that murder the innocent, a heart that hatches evil plots, feet that race down a wicked track, a mouth that lies under oath, a troublemaker in the family. Psalm 133 verse 1 says, "How good and pleasant it is when brothers live together in unity."

Listen to me, demons. It is God's will that I dwell in peace with my family members. In the name of Jesus, I rebuke, bind, and destroy the powers of all family-breaking demons, who have decided to put enmity, confusion, and trouble between me and my spouse; between me and my children; between me and my relatives. Break, be loosed, and be gone, I command in the name of Jesus. Amen.

Heavenly Father, in the most peace loving name of our Lord Jesus Christ, my God, my Lord and Master, and by the power of the Holy Spirit, I cover all my family relations with the protective power in the blood of Jesus Christ of Nazareth.

I cover my brothers and sisters, my in-laws, my parents, my uncles and aunts, my grandparents, my great grandparents, my godparent, and all my family ties with the sanctifying blood of Jesus. My mouth will speak words of wisdom; the utterance from my heart will give understanding (Psalm 49:3).

Heavenly Father, God of love, where there is hurt, let there be forgiveness, healing, and restoration, and above all let Your grace, mercy, favor and blessings abound to thy glory. In the name of Jesus Christ of Nazareth, I pray. Amen

## O Lord Bless My Husband
### (To be prayed by wives for husbands)

Heavenly Father, Jehovah Shalom, in the agape loving name of my Lord Jesus Christ, I thank You for my husband (mention name), that he loves me; he is affectionate and sympathetic and patient with me.

I believe in Jesus' name that he is compassionate, not harsh, bitter, or resentful toward me, because he loves and cherishes me, in a sense, as his own body (Colossians 3:19 AMP). May the favor of the Lord our God rest upon him. Establish the work of his hands, and yes establish the work of his hands (Psalm 90:17).

Heavenly Father, I thank You that because You watch Your Word to perform it, Your Word is working in our marriage. My husband (mention name) will never be attracted to or infatuated with a loose women, embrace the bosom of an outsider, or go astray (Proverbs 5:20). I declare and decree, in the marriage-binding name of Jesus Christ of Nazareth. So let it be done!

## Demons of Confusion

In the powerful name of our Lord Jesus Christ, my God, my Lord and Master, my Deliverer and Protector, Heavenly Father, Jehovah-Nissi, Jehovah Shalom, I bind all demons of confusion, that have been causing trouble between me and my spouse, between me and my friends, between me and my in-laws, between me and my parents, between me and my siblings, between me and my co-workers, between me and my supervisors, and between people known and unknown to me.

I command you to cease your activities in the name of Jesus.

I replace your troubles with love, peace, and respect in the loving and compassionate name of Jesus Christ of Nazareth. Amen.

## O Lord, Bless My Wife
**(To be prayed by husbands for wives)**

I thank You, Heavenly Father, that my wife (mention name) loves, respects and reverences me. She notices, regards, honor, prefers, venerates, and esteems me. She defers to me, praises me, loves and admires me exceedingly (Ephesians 5:33 AMP).

She will comfort, encourage, and do me only good as long as there is life in her. She is intelligent and a virtuous woman, she is far more precious than jewels, and her value is far more above rubies or pearls. She opens her mouth with skillful and godly wisdom.

In her tongue is the law of kindness, giving counsel and instruction. The bread of idleness (gossip, discontent, and self-pity) she will not eat (Proverbs 31).

Father, I thank and praise You that You watch Your Word to perform it and that Your Word is working in our marriage. Our lives have been transformed into the image of Jesus, by the renewal of our minds. In the name of Jesus Christ of Nazareth I pray. Amen.

## Demons Assigned to Interfere with my Marriage

In the powerful name of our Lord Jesus Christ, my God, my Lord and Master, Heavenly Father, Jehovah-Nissi, Jehovah Shalom, I bind all demonic spirits that are monitoring and policing my marriage.

Those who would not let my true marriage partner come to me or have been pushing unsuitable partners, into my life. I rebuke and bind them. I destroy, and render null and void every curse of lack of marriage, divorce or barrenness in my life. In the name of Jesus, I destroy all such curses in my life, and the life of my seed and future generations. God has heard my cry and will send my true spiritual partner, and my marriage will glorify Him in the name of Jesus, I pray. Amen.

# Family Well-Being

## Demons that have been assigned to fight against my Family, hear me and obey!

### Family-Wreaking Demons

In the most wonderful, care-loving name of our Lord Jesus Christ, Heavenly Father, Jehovah-Nissi, Jehovah-Jireh, Jehovah Shalom, I come against every demon that has been assigned to oppress, steal, fight, destroy, and kill my family members (mention their names) this year.

In the name of Jesus Christ of Nazareth, I bind you, demons. I cancel and nullify your assignments against us. I render them null and void. I cripple and destroy your powers.

Listen to me, you demons. My spouse and children are under the covering of the blood of Jesus. Jesus is the head of my household. We are heirs of the most high God, through Jesus Christ. We are His kings, and we are His priests today. My home is blessed. The works of my hands are blessed. We have peace, love, and joy from the Holy Spirit. Father, I thank You that You speak and declare the truth (Isaiah 45:19).

Father, I thank You that You watch Your Word to perform it according to Jeremiah 1:12. Thank You in the name of Jesus. Amen.

Heavenly Father, Jehovah Adonai, Jehovah Tsidqenu, El-Shaddai, Jehovah Shalom, in the precious name of our Lord Jesus Christ, my God, my Lord and Master, I thank You that my marriage is sanctified. I bind any demon of marital infidelity operating in our marriage.

Any spirit of lust, fornication, adultery, homosexuality, or sexual perversion assigned to wreck my marriage and destroy our lives, I bind you. I break your powers. I curse you. I cast you out of our lives and our marriage. Break and go, and don't come back! May the consuming fire of the Holy Spirit torment you if you don't leave now.

Father, release Your blessings and anointing on my marriage as a sign of Your goodness and tender mercies. In the name of Jesus I pray. Amen.

## Desolate Homes

In the gracious name of our Lord Jesus Christ, my Savior, my Lord and Master, Heavenly Father, Jehovah Rohi, El-Shaddai, Jehovah Jireh, Jehovah Shalom, Jehovah Shammah, I come against any spirit of disobedience, anger, rebellion, lying, cheating, spirit of stubbornness, pride, selfishness, and any foul spirits that may be operating in my family to cause trouble, dissension, and bitterness to render my home desolate.

Lord Jesus, my righteousness is from You, the head of my household. It shall be well with my soul. The Holy Spirit is my Helper Mentor, Teacher and Comforter. My household shall bear fruits of the Spirit.

Our house shall be full of love, joy, peace, patience, kindness, goodness, faithfulness, gentleness, and self-control (Galatians 5:22-23).

Thank You, Heavenly Father, that our children obey us. I thank You that as they honor us, their parents, it shall be well with their souls, and they will live long on the earth in the name of Jesus, I pray. Amen.

## Unsaved Family Members

Heavenly Father, Jehovah Adonai, Jehovah Jireh, El-Shaddai, Jehovah Shalom, in the precious name of our Lord Jesus Christ, my Savior, my Lord and Master, I bind any spirit that is fighting against the salvation of my family members (mention names).

Lord Jesus, I bind and break the powers of all spiritual thieves who have been stealing Your Word from my loved ones (Matthew 13:19). I come against the god of this world, Satan, who has blinded them from seeing the need for Your saving grace (2 Corinthians 4:4).

Lord Jesus, I stand on Your promise that if I believe in You, my household and I will be saved. Father, as I have believed, I know that my loved ones are saved.

Lord Jesus, I thank You for Your command to go into the world and make disciples of all nations. Based on this mandate, I thank You that You have saved the souls that I have mentioned.

They have been born again by Your Spirit. Holy Spirit, help them walk uprightly, not according to the ways of the world, the lust of the eyes, the pride of life, and sinful hearts, to gratify the lust of the flesh.

Father, in the name of Jesus, I bind any evil spirit that might lay claim to my children. I cancel any ancestral covenant, initiation, debt, and curse that may have come upon them through my parents or my wife's family line.

Father, please forgive any ancestral sins that have become a curse, ten generations on both side of the family. In the "can do" name of Jesus I pray. Amen.

## Demons of Peer Pressure

In the merciful and gracious name of our Lord Jesus Christ, my Savior, my Lord and Master, Heavenly Father, Jehovah Rohi, El-Shaddai, Jehovah Jireh, Jehovah Shalom, I come against any contrary spirit posing as my children's best friends to lead them astray or into temptation.

I raise a Holy Spirit triple standard against the spirit of temptation called peer pressure, in whatever form, wherever it may be found, and whenever it chooses to manifest itself.

Father, in the name of Jesus Christ of Nazareth, deliver my children from the hour of evil and temptation that is coming upon the world, for Yours is the kingdom, and the power, and the glory forever, and ever (Revelation 7:12) Amen.

## Spiritual Enforcers

Heavenly Father, Jehovah-Nissi, Jehovah Shalom, in the precious name of our Lord Jesus Christ, my God, my Lord and Master, Contend, O LORD, with those who contend with me; fight against those who fight against me (Psalm 35:1)

Father, I take authority based on Your Word, and I bind any demonic interference to change or delay what You have purposed for my children.

You evil spirit assigned to enforce any curse on my children, no matter your office or rank in the spiritual realm, I bind you. I break your powers. I cast you out of their lives. My Heavenly Father has put a wall of fire around them. They are under the covering of the blood of Jesus. I loose the anointing of the Holy Spirit in their lives. The anointing that breaks yokes and curses and lifts burdens as per Isaiah 10:27. My children are blessed, in the name and glory of the Father, the Son, and by the power of the Holy Spirit, world without end, Amen.

Heavenly Father, Jehovah Nissi, Jehovah Shalom, in the precious name of our Lord Jesus Christ, my God, my Lord and Master, I stand on Your promise that my children are Your heritage to me (Psalm 127:3). I am fully persuaded that they are blessed with all manner of spiritual blessings in the spiritual realm according to Ephesians 1:3.

They will be the head and not the tail; they will lend and not borrow (Deuteronomy 28:13). Father, I commit their minds, intellect, wisdom, and studies to Your care.

I bind any demonic attempt or interference to harass them at school, on the recreational grounds, and in any activities connected with their education and life.

Father, may we not lack the financial means to send them to school. Heavenly Father, let Your divine favor, favor before God and man, operate in the lives of my children, my nieces and nephews, grandchildren, godchildren, and all children entrusted to my care.

Father, bless them and use them as a point of contact to bless other children. In the name of Jesus Christ of Nazareth, I pray. Amen.

## Spiritual Marriages

In the powerful name of our Lord Jesus Christ, my God, my Lord and Master, my Deliverer and Protector, Heavenly Father, Jehovah Nissi, Jehovah Shalom, I bind all demons of spiritual marriages. My children will not be married to any demons. I bind and cast out any demons, and any evil chief spirit laying claim to my children from my family background.

I reject and cast out any false and troublesome suitors as prospective mates, or partners for my children.

Gracious Father, please send their ordained partners, and when it is time for them to be married, let them seek Your face on this matter. Holy Spirit, Your Excellency, empower them to be sensitive to Your warnings, and guidance in their lives. In Jesus name, I pray. Amen.

## Transgender Demons

Heavenly Father, Jehovah Nissi, Jehovah Shalom, in the precious name of our Lord Jesus Christ, my God, my Lord and Master, my Deliverer and Protector, and by the power of the Holy Spirit, I rebuke, bind and break the powers of all demons who have been assigned to interfere with the reproductive organs or the sexual orientation of my children and have vowed to cut off my seed. I rebuke and cast out all gender-bender spirits.

I break all curses that have been placed on their reproductive organs. Demons, listen to me. It is God's will that I multiply, and my seed after me. May the fire of the Holy Spirit consume you if you dare attempt to interfere in any way, shape, or form to harass their bodies, marriages or welfare.

Father, I entrust them (mention their names) to Your care. If their marriages or their reproductive organs have been sold or damaged, please send Your angels to retrieve them or give them new ones. In the name of Jesus, I pray.

## Heavenly Father, Bless Our Children

In the merciful and gracious name of our Lord Jesus Christ, my Savior, my Lord and Master, Heavenly Father, Jehovah Rohi, El-Shaddai, Jehovah Jireh, Jehovah Shalom, I thank You that You have poured Your Spirit upon my seed and Your blessings upon my children.

Father, help us we the parents to teach Your Word diligently, when we sit in our house or walk by the way, when we lie down or rise up. Heavenly Father, let Your divine visitation and favor be upon the children, and let Your anointing flow in their lives; give them hearts of flesh and write Your laws on their hearts.

Father, give them a spirit of boldness and power and sound mind. Father, give them Your peace. Father, as You are Holy, let them be Holy. Let them know the difference between the holy and the profane, and let them become a vessel of honor fit for the Master's use and to serve Him faithfully to the end. In the name of Jesus, I pray. Amen.

## Give Thanks

I thank You, Heavenly Father. I thank You, Jesus. I thank You, Holy Spirit for Your visitation, and for having won the victory for me. In the name of Jesus I pray. Amen

## The Grace

May the grace of our Lord Jesus Christ, the love of God, and the sweet fellowship of the Holy Spirit be with me now and forever.

Surely angels of goodness and mercy shall follow me all the days of my life, and I will dwell in the house of the Lord forever and ever. in Jesus name I pray.

# Amen

# References

Brown, Rebecca, MD, *Prepare for War.* Springdale, PA: Whitaker House, 1987.

Brown, Rebecca MD, He Came To Set The Captives Free, Chick Publications, Chino, Calif., 1986.

Ing, Richard, *Spiritual Warfare.* New Kensington, PA: Whitaker House, 1996.

Murillo, Mario, *I am the Christian the Devil Warned You About.* Danville, CA: Fresh Fire Communications, 1996.

Ofoegbu, Mike, *Dangerous Prayers Part 1-4.* Lagos State, Nigeria: Holy Ghost Anointed Books Ministries, 1998.

Olukoya, D. K., Dr.; *Prayer Rain.* . Lagos, Nigeria: Mountain of Fire and Miracles Ministries, 1999.

Robeson, Jerry and Carol, *Strongman's His Name...What's His Game?* New Kensington, PA: Whitaker House, 1985.

Adams, R. J, *Angels and Revelations.* http://www.rjatropical.com/WEB2003/ang20html.

Androphile Gay History Project: The World History of Male Love.

Copyleft © 2004, Androphile Project. www.androphile.org/.

*CNN Presents*: "Infidelity." Aired December 21, 2003.

CBS *60 Minutes*: "Porn in the U.S.A"; Aired September 5, 2004.

Grantley, Morris, *Premarital Sex Re-examined.* www.net-burst.net/ singles/premarital.htm, February 2005

Knox, Noelle, "Nordic family ties don't mean tying the knot." *USA TODAY*, December 16, 2004.

Crary, David, "Bible Belt Leads U.S. in Divorces," *Associated Press,* November 12, 1999.

Rosen, Margery D. *"Can this marriage be saved?"* He's a Sportsaholic, She says: he watches too much tube. He says: she's too needy." by MSN 2004. www.women.msn.com

Rainey, Dennis "Is there hope for a lasting Marriage?" www.everystudent.com. 1999.

Advice with Dr. Dee "Cohabitation Before Marriage : High Divorce Rate." http://www.drdaveanddee.com/cohabitation.html

Al Cooper, PhD (Cert. Sex therapist) *Sexploration.* "Scoring On and Off the Court: Why star athletes so frequently end up in sex scandal." http://www.msnbc.msn.com/id/3076598/ November 04, 2003

Chandni Jhunjhunwala *"Is your marriage ripe for an affair?"* http:// lhj.com/lhj/story.jhtml?storyid=/templatedata/lhj/story/data/IsYourMa rriageRipeforAnAffair_09012004.xml&categoryid=/templatedata/lhj/ category/data/MarriageBasics.xml&page=3 December 2004.

Robinson, B.A. *US Divorce Rate*: *For various faith groups, age groups, & geographic areas* Copyright © 2000 to 2004 by Ontario Consultants on Religious Tolerance. Originally written: April 27, 2000. - http://www.religioustolerance.org

Linscott, Rosa. "The Traditionalist and Libertarian Views of Sexual Morals". http://www.umm.maine.edu/resources/beharchive/bexstudents/RosaLinscott/rl360.html.

The *Oprah Winfrey* show: "Born in the Wrong Body?" From the show *The 11-Year-Old Who Wants a Sex Change* Aired May 12, 2004.

The *Oprah Winfrey* show "What Your Marriage is Trying to Teach You." Aired December 06, 2001.

The *Oprah Winfrey* show "Teen Dating abuse." Aired April 17, 2003.

The *Oprah Winfrey* show "Inside prison: Why women murder." Aired June 17, 2004.

Munsy, Phil Pastor. *Crown.* Men's Bible Conference Faith Fellowship Ministry, Sayreville, NJ, March 2, 2002.

The *Oprah Winfrey* show: "Is Your Child Living a Double Life?" Aired October 02, 2003. For more information on the movie *Thirteen*, visit www.apple.com/trailers/fox_searchlight/thirteen/

Ball, Aimee Lee "She's come undone: How does a smart woman get lost in a relationship-and find herself again? The *Oprah* magazine, September 2004.

"The Secret of Family Happiness." Watch Tower Bible and Tract Society of Pennsylvania. Watch Tower Bible and Tract Society of New York, Inc., 1996.

*Answers to tough questions.* "Reaching out to pornography addicts and the people who love them." Fires of Darkness Ministries. http://www.firesofdarkness.com. November 2004.

"Narcissism Personality Disorder," November 2004 www.healthyplace.com/communities/personality_Disorders.

CBS News Early Report (Early Show) "Where Is God?"
http://www.cbsnews.com/earlyshow/healthwatch/healthnews/
20010913terror_spiritual.shtm. September 13, 2001.

Spock, Benjamin. *The Reader's Companion to American History.*
http://college.hmco.com/history/readerscomp/rcah/html/ah_
081200_spockbenjami.htm.

*"Benjamin Spock, Physician Heal Thyself."* Vision Journal. Cited
November 2004. http://www.vision.org/jrnl/0006/bvbspock.html

"Prison," Microsoft® Encarta® Online Encyclopedia 2005
http://encarta.msn.com © 1997-2005 Microsoft Corporation.

Divorce Magazine, *U.S. Divorce Statistics* Copyright © 1996-2005
http://www.divorcemag.com/statistics/statsUS.shtml

*Associated Press.* "More unmarried women having children"-
October 28, 2005. © *2005.*

Ayanna "The Exploitation of Women in Hip-hop Culture" My
Sistahs © 2001, Advocates for Youth 10/20/2005 http://www.
mysistahs.org/features/hiphop.htm

Cnn.com-McCready to Oprah: I'm still healing November 4,
2005. http://www.cnn.com/2005/SHOWBIZ/Music/11/04/people.
mindymccready.ap/index.html

## *A Must-Have Addition To Your Collections*

This Spiritual Warfare Prayer Book contains spiritual gold nuggets to revolutionize your prayer life.

Approx: 124pgs

## Table Of Contents

Introduction
A: The Power of Your Words (Adapted from Target or Weapon)
B: Praise and Worship (Adapted from Target or Weapon)
C: The Sinner's Prayer
D: Warfare Prayers:


**Opening Prayers: Give Thanks**
  **Family**
Give Thanks In All Things
Jesus Christ The Same Yesterday, And To Day, And For Ever
Joy Of Fellowship
The Power Of His Name
Prayer Answering God
Merciful God
The Power Of The Blood Of Jesus
He Is Worthy
The Presence Of The Holy Spirit

# About the Author

Ebenezer Gyasi was raised as a Presbyterian. In college, he was a member of Campus Crusade for Christ, a college evangelical group devoted to training and making disciples on campus. After college he became actively involved in his local congregation as a Sunday school teacher, an Elder, Clerk of Session, and a member of the Stephen's Ministry, a group of lay preachers within the congregation. His life was turned upside down after the September 11, 2001, tragedy. In his search for a deeper spiritual life, he was introduced to the Deliverance ministry, where he saw first hand the power of God to heal and set people free from demonic strongholds. He realized that God can use anybody who avails himself for His vineyard. The *Target or Weapon* and *Deliverance-On-The-Go* spiritual warfare series are testimonies to what God has done with his spiritual life.

Printed in the United States
52003LVS00002B/103-165

9 781420 868951